ALBRIGHT

The Life and Times of JOHN J. ALBRIGHT

MARK GOLDMAN

BUFFALO
HERITAGE
PRESS

Buffalo Heritage Press
266 Elmwood Avenue, #407
Buffalo, NY 14222
www.BuffaloHeritage.com

Book design by Goulah Design Group, Inc.

FRONT COVER: John J. Albright fishing at Wilmurt, his Adirondack
retreat. Photograph by Susan Fuller Albright, circa 1910.
Copyright Albright Family, 1910. All rights reserved

ISBN: 978-1-942483-34-2 (softcover)
ISBN: 978-1-942483-35-9 (hardcover)

Library of Congress control number available upon request.

Printed in the U.S.A.

10 9 8 7 6 5 4 3 2 1

Contents

Acknowledgments

Despite the involvement of John J. Albright in just about every aspect of life in turn-of-the-century Buffalo, I have discovered only three documents that suggest that "he was there." The first is a paving contract signed by Albright, his two partners and Grover Cleveland, Buffalo's mayor, in 1882. The second is the letter that he wrote in 1900 in which he announced his historic gift to the Buffalo Society of Artists, the Albright Art Gallery. The third is a letter, signed by him in 1918, in which he politely declined to serve another term on the board of the Society. That's it. His "fingers" were in everything: coal, steel, electrical power, banking and philanthropy. Yet his "finger prints" are nowhere to be found. No notes, no diaries, no correspondence; not even with E.B. Green, the incredible architect who did so much work with and for Albright. The correspondence between Darwin Martin and Frank Lloyd Wright is voluminous. Yet between Albright and Green there is nothing: not a note from Albright nor an invoice from Green.

It's not as if I haven't looked. My efforts to find primary material and information have led me far and wide. I have searched repeatedly and extensively and have exhausted the patience of librarians at the Buffalo History Museum and at the Grosvenor Room at the Buffalo and Erie County Public Library. I have made diligent efforts to glean all that I could from the remarkable Internet-based archives at www.buffaloresearch.com and in www.Buffaloah.com. My curiosity about Albright's alleged ties to the Van Sweringen brothers of Cleveland has led me to travel to the Western Reserve Historical Society. For his connections to the Langdons, I have visited the Chemung Valley History Museum in Elmira. For his origins in the coal business, I went to the Albright Memorial Library in Scranton. For the Albright family's intriguing interest in photography, I have spent hours, accompanied by two generations of Albright grandchildren, Rob and Liz Hawley, in the collections department at the George Eastman House in Rochester, New York. And for an insight into the dynamics of the family I visited the Countway Library at Harvard University, home to the papers of Fuller Albright, M.D. I have sought out and met with the many patient and helpful members of the Albright family: Lorny and Liz Hurd in East Aurora, New York; Sandra Stubbs in Rochester, New York; Rob Hawley in Syracuse, New York; Susan Fuller Parker in Cazenovia, New York; David F. Albright in Cambridge, Massachusetts; and Nancy Schleuter and Mary Albright in Princeton, New Jersey.

I owe my greatest personal thanks to John Albright's grandson Birge Albright. Although Birge knew neither his grandmother Susan Fuller Albright nor his grandfather John J. Albright, Birge is a serious student of history with a deep interest in his family. It was this that led him as a senior at Harvard University to research and to write the three-part essay that I reference regularly throughout this biography. Over the course of this work Birge has become a friend. I have particularly fond recollections of my meetings with him at his home in Cambridge and at "The Chalet" at Wilmurt. He has played an inspirational role in this work.

For those of us who write history, nobody is more worthy of expressions of gratitude than reference librarians. Ours in Buffalo are extraordinary and I want to thank each of them:

At the Archives of the Albright-Knox Art Gallery, Gabrielle Carlo is a passionate and tireless archivist deeply committed to the mission of the Gallery and the importance of the Archives to the life of that institution. She was an invaluable colleague and together we worked to reveal the mystery of John J. Albright.

At the Buffalo History Museum, Cynthia Van Ness, Shane Stephenson and Amy Miller.

At the Grosvenor Room at the Buffalo and Erie County Public Library, Amy Pickard, Chuck Alaimo, Rhonda Konig, Sue Catrona and Andrew Maines.

At the Niagara Falls Ontario Public library, Cathy Roy, the local history librarian. At the Erie County Clerk's office I was helped by Jan Borman. Rebecca Diina Lacivita helped me decipher the complexities of the public records that are housed in the Surrogate's Court.

At the George Eastman Museum I was helped by Rachel Andrews, Assistant Collections Manager, Department of Photography. Douglas Levere of Print Collection Buffalo helped me to find the fabulous Puck cartoon referenced in the text.

Clinton Brown, Buffalo architect and preservationist, helped me better understand the changes that have occurred over time to the Albright Estate on W. Ferry Street. Brian Baird helped me interpret the codicils to Albright's will. Irene Sipos offered a very helpful early reading of the manuscript. Rob McElroy helped me understand the workings of "the Kodak," Eastman's first camera, the one Raymond K. Albright took with him on the Albright family's 1888 Grand Tour. Margaret Milliron provided essential help during the early conceptual phases of this work. Ramona Whitaker spent many hours perfecting the text.

I am deeply appreciative of the support for The Albright Weekend that has been provided by The Baird Foundation, the Robert & Patricia Colby Foundation, the Mulroy Family Foundation and the Carlos & Elizabeth Heath Foundation.

The person to whom I owe the greatest thanks is Marti Gorman of Buffalo Heritage Press. Marti is a terrific editor, a tireless publisher and a passionate Buffalonian who does wonderful work in and for our community.

Introduction

When I first arrived in Buffalo, the name that I heard more than any other was "Albright," as in "The Albright." Although it had been officially known as "the Albright-Knox Art Gallery" since 1962, the museum of modern and contemporary art built in 1905 and named for its original benefactor, John J. Albright, was always simply referred to as The Albright. "I'll meet you at the Albright." "Are you going to the 'Festival of the Arts Today' at the Albright?" "Did you hear Lucas Foss last night at the Albright?" That, notwithstanding the extraordinary gratitude all knew was owed to Seymour H. Knox II, scion of the F. W. Woolworth Company founder, Buffalo philanthropist, and noted art patron, who spearheaded the 1962 expansion of the gallery. While over the years people increasingly became comfortable with the hyphenated "Albright-Knox," the simple, shorthand moniker for the gallery remained "the Albright."

Carnegie Hall, the Morgan Library, the Rockefeller Institute were vaunted institutions named for people about whom everybody knew at least something. But "The Albright"? Seymour Knox, an endearing figure known affectionately to many as "Shorty," was still very much alive, a living, breathing part of the daily life of the city. It was hard not to be aware and appreciative of Knox's role in the cultural life of the community, the fact that it was he who was responsible for the elegant black-glass jewel box that housed his remarkable collection. But Albright? Few knew and few were curious about Albright, who he was and why this extraordinary gallery in this fascinating city that I had come to call home bore his name.

Gradually, as I learned more about the history of Buffalo, I came to learn that it was John J. Albright, in fact, who was among those responsible for the three most transformative events in the twentieth-century history of the city: the move to Buffalo of the company that would become the Lackawanna Steel Company; the hosting in Buffalo of the Pan-American Exposition in 1901; and, most extraordinary of all, that it was his vision and his generosity that led to the creation of the city's most significant cultural institution, The Albright-Knox Art Gallery. John J. Albright was, without question, the most creative and powerful person in the life of the city in his time.

Over the years I have found no more revealing, exciting, and enticing source of information about Buffalo's history than the Scrapbook Collection housed in the Grosvenor Room at the Buffalo and Erie County Public Library. This collection, covering several hundred square feet of shelf space, was started in 1900 by Sara Palmer Sheldon, the then-director of the library's Newspaper Room. Following her retirement in 1932, the job of scouring through local newspapers to locate, clip, and sort articles into scrapbooks, each covering a different subject, fell to other staff members. The scrapbooks, each with its own name: Buffalo's Foreign Population, Art, Theater and Concert Halls,

Churches, Trees, Schools, Homes, and so on, are filled with endlessly engaging stories of people, places, and events in the history of Buffalo.

One day in the fall of 2015, while I was casually flipping through the pages of the volume marked "Homes," I came across a news item that stopped me in my tracks. "Auction Gavel to Sweep Albright Mansion Clean" read one headline. Then another: "Sell Albright House Tonight: Mansion itself, stripped of all its art treasures, goes under auctioneer's hammer." The Albright home, I knew, was not a simple house but rather an enormous homestead located in the middle of almost a square block between Elmwood Avenue to the west, Delaware to the east, and Ferry and Cleveland to the south and north. The twelve acres of land on which it was located contained greenhouses, tennis courts, stables, and, the centerpiece, the spectacular mansion, modeled by one of Buffalo's greatest architects, Edward B. Green, after "St. Catherine's Court," one of the great Tudor homes in Bath, England. All of this up for auction? All of this destined for demolition? What had happened and how?

The materials housed in the Grosvenor Room and the librarians who work there are among the great treasures of Western New York. They quickly led me to another source, *Niagara Frontier,* a long-extinct journal dedicated to local history. The index of the journal contained two references to "Albright." The first was a small announcement tucked away in the back of a 1954 volume: "Mr. Birge Albright, grandson of John J. Albright, who gave the Albright Art Gallery to the city of Buffalo, is assembling material for a biography of his grandfather and would like to get

Five of the ten albums that contain Susan Fuller Albright's photographs of the Albright family.

These albums are owned by and used with the permission of the Albright family

in touch with anyone having documents or personal letters from him."[1]

Birge Albright, I subsequently learned, had been a senior at Harvard and a serious student of history who, at the urging of his father, Dr. Fuller Albright, chose to write as his senior honors thesis a biography of his grandfather, John J. Albright. With this in mind, Birge moved to Buffalo in the summer of 1955. Staying sometimes at The Lenox Hotel, sometimes with family and friends in Buffalo and East Aurora, Birge spent the bulk of his time in the Grosvenor Library. In the large, circular main reading room (the library had been built originally as a velodrome) still housed in its own magnificent building at the corner of Franklin and Edward streets, he pored over microfilmed newspapers, crinkled city directories, and atlases. He also spent entire days at what was then called the Buffalo Historical Society, diligently piecing together a story that began in Scranton, Pennsylvania, in the middle of the nineteenth century and ended in Buffalo in 1931. Between 1960 and 1962, his biography, a three-part essay, appeared in the pages of *Niagara Frontier*. It was to this essay that I was directed when sixty years later I began to write my own biography of a man who is perhaps the most important person in the history of the city of Buffalo.

Birge Albright's essay is a comprehensive, largely chronological study that covers the highlights of John J. Albright's life: his role in bringing to Buffalo the company that became Bethlehem Steel; how he helped to create the fantastical, magical kingdom of the Pan-American Exposition; that he saw the potential of and helped harness the power of Niagara Falls; and, as his magnificent gift of the Albright Art Gallery to the city of Buffalo so powerfully demonstrates, that he knew and understood the boundless power of art.

But Birge Albright's thorough chronological account did not reveal what John Albright thought and felt about all that he did. Who were his friends? What about his extraordinary relationship with E. B. Green? What motivated him to commission the Albright Art Gallery? And how did he respond to its increasingly modernist direction? What about those two magical mystery tours of Europe and Egypt that Birge Albright tells us his grandfather took, each lasting many months? Did he keep a diary? Did he send postcards home? And what about his family: his two wives and eight children? Who were they and what was the nature of their relationship with the great man? What about those seemingly tragic end days when house, home, and all its contents were unceremoniously liquidated? What had happened? How had this powerful man, whose actions and ideas shaped twentieth-century Buffalo, fallen on such hard times?

And who, indeed, was Birge Albright? Was he alive? Could I find him? Would he talk to me? I learned through either his cousin Lorny Albright in East Aurora, New York, or his niece Susan Stubbs in Rochester, New York, that Birge Albright lived in Cambridge, Massachusetts. I found his telephone number. Nervous and a bit hesitant, I called. "Yes, of course. By all means, please come visit me in Cambridge. We will have much to talk about." And so, in the fall of 2015 I found myself in a modest, 1920s brick apartment building minutes from Harvard Square, in the warm and welcoming company of Birge Albright. "Dante" had found his "Virgil," the guide who would help me wend my way through the *selva oscura* of the life of John J. Albright.

Birge is in his mid-eighties, a retired lawyer and an avid student of history. He attends classes at Harvard University two days every week. The densely packed book shelves in his apartment are filled with many of the same serious tomes that fill mine: biographies of the presidents, historical interpretations of Supreme Court decisions; histories of nations and cities, of art and music and literature. Birge is witty, erudite, pleasant and engaging, and we hit it off immediately. "Sit down," he said gently, handing me an old album filled with pages and pages of black and white photographs. "These were taken by my grandmother, Susan—Susan Fuller Albright, JJA's [second] wife." George Eastman [who invented the roll-film camera and founded the Eastman Kodak Company] gave her a camera in 1900," he explained. "She loved that camera and took hundreds of pictures 'til the day she died twenty-eight years later. There are eight more of these albums. The albums are at Wilmurt. Come to Wilmurt and I'll show them to you."

"Wilmurt," I had learned, was the Albright family's summer home, high on a mountain overlooking a pristine Adirondack lake, inaccessible during the winter months. Rather than wait for summer to see Susan Albright's photographs, so critical to my work, the exact lens into the world of John J. Albright that I so eagerly sought, Birge came up with a solution. "Go to Syracuse," he advised. "Go see my second cousin Rob Hawley. He has them. He's copying them all."

Robert Hawley, one of John J. Albright's great-grandchildren, is a professional photographer who, with his father and now his daughter, has owned and operated a photography studio in Syracuse, New York, since the mid-1940s. A somewhat grizzled veteran of the Vietnam War, Rob has his own stories to tell. But it was Susan Fuller Albright's photos that he wanted me to see, all of the eight leather-bound photo albums filled with hundreds of black and white photos that document the life and times of John and Susan Albright. Any student of history, let alone this one who for so many years has been fascinated by photography and the stories that photographs reveal, would have been thrilled by what Rob Hawley showed me. With her ever-present camera, Susan Fuller Albright followed the family everywhere, capturing every step of the Albright family's life-journey. She took pictures of their homes—at 730 W. Ferry Street in Buffalo, at Jekyll Island, Georgia; at Wilmurt in the Adirondacks; and at Susan's family home in Western Massachusetts. She took spectacular photos documenting the more than year-long voyage the family took to Europe in 1912. And everywhere there were pictures of their children, dozens of them, of Albright's children with his first wife, Harriet: Raymond, Ruth and Langdon; and of her children with "Joe," Susan's nickname for her husband: John J. Jr., Betty, Fuller, Nancy and Susan. These five children fill the frames of Susan's fertile camera and it is through her warm, sensitive, and artistic images of them and the world that they lived in that we can best learn about John J. Albright and his family.

Rob Hawley was excited by my efforts to chronicle the life of his great-grandfather and, with the support of other members of the large, disparate members of the Albright clan, copied each and every photograph onto a disk, which he then gave to me for my use.

Birge, Zen-like, monitored my progress, slowly and carefully revealing the nooks and crannies where the hidden fragments of the Albright family history were stored. He dropped hints and leads at varying intervals. Sometimes weeks and months passed between them. First there were the photographs taken by his grandmother, Susan Fuller Albright. Then, much later, came a casual but clear reference to a journal, a memoir written by his aunt, John Albright's youngest daughter, Susie. "Read *The Simple Life*. It will help you understand my grandmother's photographs," urged Birge. Then, weeks later, another admonition: "Aunt Susie wrote another memoir, you know," revealed Birge during a phone conversation. "It's about Jekyll Island. Read it. It will help you understand the family better." Then, in the spring of 2017 as my research was winding down, came the last of his almost-whispered instructions. "My grandmother wrote letters to my father, Fuller Albright. There are hundreds of them. Go to the Countway Library at Harvard. Read them. Get back to me and tell me what you find."

The more I learned about the life and times of John J. Albright, the more I came to realize this story was Greek in its proportions, a story of power and pathos, a story with many questions and few answers, and thus fraught with mystery. The more I learned, the more I talked with Birge and the other members of the extended Albright family, the more I felt compelled to tell the whole tale. The effort to do so has led me on the most challenging and interesting, joyous and gratifying journey of historical discovery that I have ever traveled. I offer you here the fruits of that journey.

ONE

Life Before Buffalo

Birge Albright tells us that the first Albright in America was Andrew Albrecht. A gunsmith, Andrew came from Germany in 1750 and settled in Lancaster County, Pennsylvania, changing his name from "Albrecht" to "Albright." By the outbreak of the Revolution, he was in business with a man named William Henry, a large-scale supplier of weapons to the Continental Army. The Albrights, as we shall see, liked to keep things in the family, and the two families—the Albrights and the Henrys—quickly became intertwined. By 1840, Albright's grand-daughter married William Henry's grandson who, in a fortuitous partnership with the Scranton brothers, George W. and Seldon T., had formed the Lackawanna Iron and Coal Company. By the middle of the century, Andrew's grandson, Joseph Jacob Albright, became an iron manufacturer in his own right, with a furnace near Natural Bridge, Virginia. It was there, in 1848, that John Joseph Albright was born. By the end of the nine-teenth century these marriages and connections, all of which emerged from the Lackawanna Valley, would lead to one of the most significant developments in the history of Buffalo and, in the process, to the transfor-mation of the nation's economy.

Coal needed to be mined and it needed to be shipped, and it was these two activities that engaged John J. Albright's father Jacob at the time of his son's birth. This work was visionary, requiring not only great knowledge of engineering but the mobilization of men and resources on a new and unprecedented scale. The coal business was also highly risky and often unstable, and it was in this atmosphere of great risk and reward that the young Albright was raised. When things were good they were very, very good and when they were not, as both the Albrights would learn, they could be very, very bad. Indeed, one year following the birth of his son John, the senior Albright went bankrupt. In a letter that revealed his feelings in ways that his son never did, he shared the deep shame of this experience. Writing to Seldon Scranton, a business partner as well as a distant cousin, the elder Albright lamented, "It is hard at my age [he was about 40 at the time] to be thrown upon the world penniless." He hoped, he said, that Seldon's wife "wouldn't be ashamed for her poor friend." So despondent was he that, despite the recent birth of his son, he seems to have contemplated suicide. "Death," he wrote, "would come as a relief."

The Scrantons, however, came quickly to his rescue, and Albright soon regained his position as a dominant figure in the industrial revolution that was remaking central Pennsylvania.[1] What Albright's son, John, knew and felt about this experience is unknown.

The Albrights remained true to their Moravian faith, enrolling their son John in a Moravian preparatory school in western Massachusetts. In 1865, he entered the Rensselaer Polytechnic Institute in Troy, New York. Founded in 1824, it was the oldest, most prestigious engineering college in the country and provided an intensely competitive academic setting with a course of study that ranged from mining and mineralogy to mechanical invention and bridge design and building. Albright graduated in 1869 with a degree in mining engineering. At RPI Albright had received a unique education while establishing relationships that would last a lifetime.

Albright was attracted to his highly competent and accomplished classmates, many of whom went on to make enormous contributions in a rapidly industrializing world. One was a man named Leffert L. Buck, a classmate despite being eleven years older than Albright. A veteran soldier, Buck spent the Civil War years as an officer in the Union Army fighting in that war's most horrific battles, including Antietam, Chancellorsville, and Gettysburg. Buck had entered RPI immediately after the war and became a civil engineer specializing in the use of steel to create arched bridge structures. In the early 1880s, he designed the Whirlpool Rapids Bridge at Niagara Falls. His best-known design was for the Williamsburg Bridge built over the East River in New York City. At 1600 feet, it was the longest bridge in the world when it was completed in 1903. [2]

Another of Albright's classmates was a man named Thomas Voorhees. In the 1880s, Voorhees became president of the Philadelphia and Reading Railroad, the company where Albright got his start in the coal business.

Albright was an active member of the RPI alumni association, serving as its president in 1899-1900. Given this leadership role, we can assume that he knew and was inspired by his better known fellow alumni: men such as George Washington Gale Ferris, Class of 1881, the engineer known for designing and building the original Ferris Wheel for the 1893 World's Columbian Exposition in Chicago; or the great Washington Roebling, Class of 1857, who, following his father's incapacitation, supervised construction of the Brooklyn Bridge. It was Roebling who reported just how difficult RPI was, how intense the commitment necessary to matriculate successfully. Indeed, Roebling reported that, of the sixty-five students who entered RPI with him, only twelve remained at graduation. And, he continued, "The few who did graduate left the school as mental wrecks." [3]

Albright was ready upon graduation to begin the work that would engage him for the rest of his life. In 1871, he moved to Harrisburg, Pennsylvania, where he met and then joined a man named Andrew Langdon to form a partnership in the business of coal transportation. Langdon, like Albright, was a scion of the coal industry, the nephew of Jervis Langdon of Elmira, New York, the leading coal merchant in the United States. Their partnership was a perfect match.

The Langdon family story, no less complex and compelling than Albright's, is well worth telling. It begins in Allegany County, New York, southeast of Buffalo, where Jervis Langdon was born, and continues in Elmira, where he moved in the early 1840s just as that small village on the Chemung River was becoming the major transportation hub on the New York-Pennsylvania border.

Like other long-isolated communities, Elmira was given new life following completion of the Erie Canal in 1825. By connecting New York City to the Great Lakes, the canal offered the town a link to a new enormous and burgeoning marketplace. The timing was perfect: a rapidly expanding supply, fueled by a rapidly expanding demand.

Getting coal out of the ground was one thing; finding a steady and reliable stream of commerce that would get it into the marketplace was another. All that was needed was the means to connect one to the other. Into this breach stepped innovative entrepreneurs and engineers who, armed with the necessary skills and education, fanned out into communities desperate for a connection to regional, national, and even international markets. Men like John B. Jervis, who started out as an "axman" working on the Erie Canal, but left a legacy that included tenure as chief engineer of three major canal projects and designer and construction supervisor of some of America's earliest railroads. In 1824, Jervis moved to Elmira as chief engineer of both the Chenango and the Delaware and Hudson canals. [4]

By 1833, desperate to reach the Erie Canal, a group of enterprising Elmira merchants had pressured the state legislature to help them build the Chemung Canal. A mere twenty miles long and barely a footnote in history (it became obsolete by 1880), the Chemung Canal, when completed, created a direct water link, however arduous to negotiate, for the movement of goods and produce via canal boat from Elmira to the southern end of Seneca Lake at Watkins Glen, New

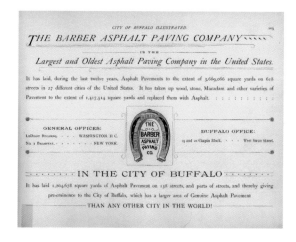

Amzi Barber, Albright's brother-in-law, encouraged Albright to move to Washington, DC to be part of the Barber Asphalt Paving Company. Barber also owned the Locomobile Company, which manufactured luxury automobiles between 1900 and 1922. Albright loved his Locomobile, even taking it with him on the family's year-long world tour in 1912. Albright was deeply loyal to Barber and in 1900 made him an offer that, much to Albright's subsequent regret, his brother-in-law could not refuse.

Reproduction by permission of the Grosvenor Room, Buffalo & Erie County Public Library, Buffalo, NY

Jervis Langdon
Chemung County Historical Society

In addition to his role as Elmira's preeminent business leader, Jervis Langdon was a moral leader in this quickly growing town on the Southern Tier. Langdon, in 1854, recruited Thomas Beecher to become the clergyman at the Park Street Presbyterian Church, which he had founded when the minister at Elmira's First Presbyterian Church refused to support the abolition of slavery. Under Langdon and Beecher, the son of reformist clergyman Lyman Beecher and half-brother of abolitionist Harriet Beecher Stowe, author of *Uncle Tom's Cabin,* Elmira, with approximately 10,000 residents had become, like nearby Rochester, a leading center of Abolitionism. Langdon's home, located across the street from the Park Street Church, became a "stop" on the Underground Railroad, where, on several occasions, Langdon entertained Frederick Douglass. [5]

York. The goal, however, was not Watkins Glen. It was the Erie Canal, and to get there still more miles needed to be traveled, still more back-breaking work needed to be done. The final link in this much-coveted but still weak-in-many-places chain was the short, challenging haul northward up Seneca Lake where canal boats, filled to the brim, mostly with coal, were pulled by manpower and horsepower all the way to Geneva, New York. Transferred again into yet another tiny but invaluable link called the Cayuga and Seneca Canal, these Elmira-based canal boats finally arrived into the great thriving center of this complex web of canals, the Erie Canal itself. Elmira merchants, those shippers and forwarders to whom national and eventually global access was so critical—people like Jervis Langdon whose coal filled so many of those over-stuffed boats—could now, finally, breathe a sigh of relief, knowing that their products were well on the way to the global market place.

By the end of the Civil War, Jervis Langdon's coal transshipment company, Langdon and Company, had become one of the largest movers of coal in the nation.

Jervis's nephew, Andrew Langdon, recognized that his future lay with his uncle and not with his father, Ledroict, the owner of a hardware store in Belmont, New York, and in the early 1870s he moved to Harrisburg, Pennsylvania, an emerging center of the coal trade. A few years after his graduation from RPI, Albright moved there, too, and in 1871 joined him to form the coal-shipping company, Langdon and Albright. Through this relationship, Albright met Andrew's sister, Harriet Langdon, whom he married in 1872.

Despite the success that Langdon and Albright were enjoying as independent coal brokers in Harrisburg, they sensed brighter horizons existed in Washington, DC. As a result of yet another canal, the Chesapeake and Ohio, the nation's capital had become a booming coal distribution center in its own right. In 1872, the brothers-in-law moved there and became agents for the Philadelphia and Reading Coal and Iron Company. In the nation's capital, John and Harriet's children, Raymond (1875), Ruth (1879), and Langdon (1880) were born. Also living there were another daughter of Ledroict Langdon, Harriet Langdon's sister Julia, and her husband, Amzi Lorenzo Barber.

Barber is a mysterious, somewhat illusive character with a varied and checkered career. Albright's relationship with him, although largely undocumented, seems to have lasted from the early 1870s until Barber died in 1909. Barber was unquestionably an intriguing character, part hero and part, it seems, flamboyant scoundrel, crusader for the education of blacks, millionaire businessman unafraid to mingle in the affairs of another country, automobile enthusiast, and yachtsman. At the turn of the century, he was owner of the *Laurena,* then the largest private yacht on the seven seas.

Who, then, was Amzi Barber and what was the nature of his relationship with John J. Albright? Barber, the son of a Congregational minister reputedly "of great strength of character," was raised in Ohio. Following his graduation from a high school in Cleveland in 1862, he enrolled in Oberlin College, beginning the first of several interesting careers. Oberlin was like no other institution of higher learning in the nation. Founded in 1833, it quickly became a hotbed of abolitionist thought and activity and, within two years of its founding, began admitting African American students. In 1837, it accepted its first group of women. Indeed, one of Barber's classmates in the Class of 1866 (three years before his soon-to-be brother-in-law John J. Albright graduated from RPI) was Mary Jane Patterson, the first African American woman in the United States to receive a college degree. Barber seems to have thrived in the heady, progressive climate of Oberlin. Upon graduating, he went immediately to work for the Freedman's Bureau in Washington, DC. The head of the bureau, a Union general named Oliver Howard, hoping to found a theological seminary for freedmen, was drawn to young Barber and asked him to join as a member of the emerging school. Quickly, though, their mission morphed, and in 1867, when Howard University was formed, dedicated to learning of "the highest grade in the Nation's capital for the colored man," Amzi Barber, as professor of natural science, was a founding faculty member. [6]

The five years that Barber taught at Howard University were exciting times to be in Washington, years when the passage of the three "slavery amendments" (the 13th, 14th, and 15th) brought hope and energy to blacks and whites everywhere longing for the fulfillment of the promise of Appomattox. Working with a racially mixed faculty and an all-black student body, Professor Barber was at the epicenter of one of the most significant periods in the nation's history. For reasons unknown to us, in 1872, five years after joining, he resigned from Howard. (Some sources indicate that Barber was acting president of the university at the time of his resignation.) On the eve of his departure, however, with his two brothers-in-law—John J. Albright and Andrew Langdon—as partners, he bought forty acres of land adjacent from Howard, and the three men entered a new phase of their lives: real estate development.

Their first venture was the development of a fifty-acre tract of land adjacent to a parcel Barber bought from Howard University in 1873. He named it "LeDroit Park" in honor of his father-in-law, Ledroict Langdon, Andrew's father in Belmont, New York. (Barber, for some reason, dropped the "c" in naming the development.)

Barber's vision for the empty land was to develop it as an exclusive residential enclave, one of the first of what would in the next century become "planned communities" and a model for suburban developments across the nation. Like those that it influenced, the houses in LeDroit Village, while offering a variety of façades, had identical floor plans and layout.

The most intriguing chapter in the LeDroit story is how Professor Barber, a graduate of Oberlin College and a member of the first faculty at the first all-black college in the country, could have, within a year of leaving that college, imagined and developed a residential neighborhood that was, when it opened, an all-white enclave, off-limits to blacks, despite its location adjacent to Howard, despite Barber's credentials as a civil rights man, and despite the climate of radical Republican opinion that dominated Washington at that time. The author of a recent book on the neighborhood writes that by the late 1870s "a fence was built around the neighborhood and guards were posted at the gates to restrain access. The fence became a point

of contention between white and black communities. Black protestors tore down the fence in July 1888, only to find it rebuilt four days later." [7] What role, if any, Albright played in the creation and management of LeDroit, given the paucity of evidence, is impossible to say. Indeed, by the time of the disturbance in 1888, Albright had been living in Buffalo, New York, for six years. Prior to his departure, Albright and Langdon joined Amzi Barber in creating a new business, one that he would take with him to Buffalo, the Barber Paving Company.

Amzi Barber was not the only charismatic person whom John J. Albright met through his marriage into the Langdon family. Through his wife, Harriet, and his brother-in-law, Andrew, Albright entered the orbit surrounding Samuel Langhorne Clemens, the writer who would soon be known to the world as "Mark Twain." In February 1870, about the time Albright met Andrew in Harrisburg, Olivia, the daughter of Jervis Langdon and the cousin of Harriet and Andrew, married Samuel Clemens. While Albright and Andrew Langdon were beginning to make their way in Harrisburg's booming coal industry, the Clemens had moved to Buffalo, where Clemens worked as an editor for *The Buffalo Express*. They lived for a year in a home on Delaware Avenue that Jervis had bought for them, but in early 1871 they returned to live with the Langdon family in Elmira.

The nature of the ties that bound the Albrights and the Clemens family is, unfortunately, unknown. The questions, though, are fascinating and beg, in the absence of answers, serious consideration. Did Albright, for example, have a relationship with Samuel

Clemens, the husband of his wife's cousin? What, if any, was the extent of the contact between them? Did the Clemenses attend the wedding of John and Harriet in 1872? Did the Albrights spend vacations with the Langdon and Clemens families in Elmira? What might have been John Albright's response to the publication in 1884 of *Huckleberry Finn*? And, finally, did Albright, who would become so generous with his growing wealth, help support his internationally celebrated in-law during the 1890s when Twain was drowning in debt?

Though tempted by Barber's visionary dreams and schemes, John Albright and his partner and brother-in-law, Andrew Langdon, were coal-men at heart. Aware of the rapidly expanding national economy, an increasingly integrated system that allowed for the creation of a global market for natural resources, John Albright and Andrew Langdon, in 1882, moved to the emerging epicenter of globalism, Buffalo, New York. It was a city that perfectly suited John J. Albright's grand visions for the future.

TWO

High Hopes in Buffalo

On the endlessly fascinating book shelves at the Old Editions Book Store in downtown Buffalo, there is a beautiful bound volume filled with high resolution photographs of Buffalo homes and factories, streets, and parks. The book, with no listed author or publisher, is simply titled *Buffalo, 1890*. Its text, as much as the photographs that accompany it, capture in elegiac prose the mood of a city that felt itself at the precipice of a historic place in time. The city as described in this book is a booming, bustling, boundless place, bursting with optimism and fueled by big dreams and high hopes. The book opens thusly: "The future of Buffalo is as hopeful and as promising as the past has been growing and prosperous." Pointing to its location, the anonymous author writes:

The site is indeed phenomenal for its growth and development. It is at the eastern terminus of lake navigation and most of the shipments by water to and from the upper lakes naturally reach the docks of Buffalo harbor. The railway traffic that comes to and goes from Buffalo is scarcely less important than the lake and canal business.

Although still heavily dependent on lake commerce, the city's economy was becoming increasingly linked to the railroads. By 1890, Buffalo was, after Chicago, the leading railroad terminus in the United States.

There were seven direct lines connecting Buffalo with six different East Coast cities; six direct lines to Chicago, Kansas City, Omaha, and St. Louis; and two direct lines between Buffalo and Pittsburgh. The New York Central was so big in Buffalo that it had its own police force.

Railroads not only linked Buffalo to the ever-growing national and global markets beyond its borders, they created greater linkages within the city, as well. In 1883, the year after Albright moved to Buffalo, the New York Central Railroad built the Belt Line Railroad, a freight and a commuter line which, by circling around the city and connecting unsettled sections, opened up whole new areas of Buffalo—Black Rock and Riverside, Central Park and the far East Side—for residential and industrial development.

With a burgeoning population—175,000 in 1880, 250,000 in 1890, and 325,000 in 1900—and a dynamically expanding economy, it was clear to John J. Albright and his brother-in-law, Andrew Langdon, that they had come to the right place at the right time, and they quickly made the most of it. By the 1880s the work that the earlier generations of Albrights and Langdons had done in Scranton and in Elmira was paying off, and Buffalo, with its sublime location, had become the preeminent port of coal transshipment in the country. The *1884 Buffalo City Directory*[1] published

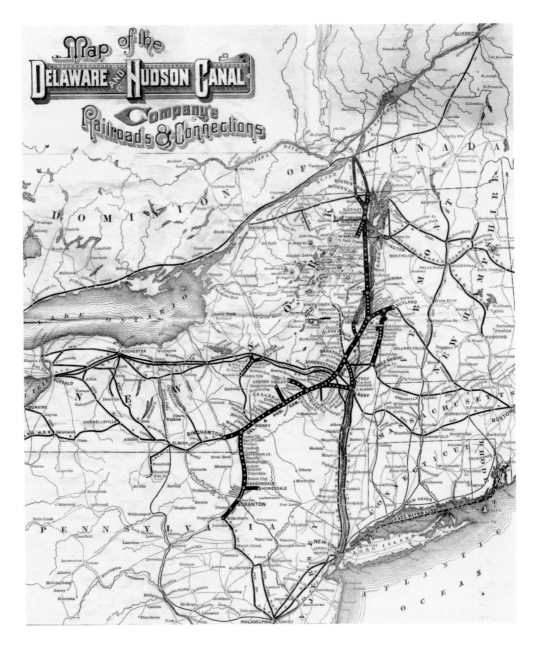

This map from the 1870s tells a powerful story about the important links and connections that canals and then railroads played in the development of Buffalo as a major port of coal transshipment.

Reproduction by permission of the Grosvenor Room, Buffalo & Erie County Public Library, Buffalo, NY

just two years after Albright and Langdon arrived in Buffalo, was filled with individuals and companies working in the business of coal transshipment. These included the Delaware, Lackawanna, and Western Railroad, which, their ad in the *Directory* noted, "keeps constantly on hand and offers for sale their Scranton coal." And there were the Delaware and Hudson Canal Company: "miners and shippers of Lackawanna coal"; the Pennsylvania Coal Company: "miners and shippers of anthracite coal"; and the Lehigh Valley Coal Company: "miners and shippers of their celebrated Wilkes Barre Coal."

Buffalo was a dynamic center of industry. There were soap companies, dominated by Larkin. Spencer-Kellogg was the leading oils and lubricants firm. There were Schoellkopf's National Aniline, Jewett Refrigeration, and giant machine shops like Buffalo Forge. A dozen or more bicycle factories, most notably that owned by George N. Pierce, who later built the luxurious "Pierce Arrow" automobile, were headquartered in Buffalo. Despite increased competition from other lake ports, in 1890 Buffalo remained a dominant center of the grain trade, its waterfront dotted with no fewer than forty-five grain elevators. Down river in Tonawanda was a gigantic lumber industry led by William A. Gratwick and brothers Charles and Frank Goodyear, all Albright colleagues. Stockyards and breweries and railroad repair shops and forges and foundries—all were here. And, to sustain the social life of the thousands of people who worked in these many varied establishments, more than 1,500 saloons could be found on streets and corners in neighborhoods all over the city. [2]

Albright and Andrew Langdon, each with at least one generation of experience in the business of coal transshipment, fit right in. By 1882, they were operating two separate coal brokerage businesses. One, known as Albright and Co., "marketed all coal going west from Buffalo." The other, with partner Thomas Guilford Smith, another Rensselaer alumnus with whom Albright did a great deal of business, was known as Albright and Smith and "handled the entire coal sold in Canada and the State of New York." [3]

Because they were middlemen, unencumbered by the crushing financial obligations of carrying large inventories or maintaining extensive infrastructure, the brokerage business was perfect for these three young men, enabling them to create enormously successful businesses without requiring access to large amounts of capital.

The work of the Albright partnerships during the 1880s transformed not only the city's economy but its landscape as well, particularly the waterfront. Railroads and coal companies were acquiring, sometimes by stealth, sometimes legitimately, large swaths of Buffalo's waterfront, which they quickly put to use for their commercial purposes. As the movement of goods shifted rapidly from canal and lake boats to railroads, the form and function of Buffalo's waterfront was radically altered. Structures of unprecedented scope and scale were being built to accommodate the city's rapidly changing economy, none more so than the gigantic railroad trestle that Albright and his partners built at the foot of Erie Street in the early 1880s.

An ingenious feat of engineering, the purpose of this enormous iron and wood structure was to allow a train filled with coal to move gradually from grade level to a place high enough that coal could be dumped into canal boats and lake steamers waiting below. The visionary work of Albright and Langdon, powered by their background and training, was reshaping not only the city's economy but, just as significantly, the look and the feel of the places where the people of Buffalo lived their daily lives.

Although the reach of the Philadelphia and Reading Railroad was already vast, Albright and Langdon expanded its length and breadth still further. By the end of the 1880s, Birge Albright reports, the P&R shipped twenty percent of the nation's coal through the harbor at Buffalo, and Albright, as a result of his contract with the company, received twenty-five cents per ton. John J. Albright had made his first million.

When Albright moved to Buffalo he brought with him his ties to Amzi Barber, particularly his partnership in the Barber Asphalt Paving Company. Concurrent with his efforts to develop Ledroit Village, Barber, who had made a careful study of how asphalt could be used in the creation of paved streets, convinced the District of Columbia that it should replace the city's decaying wooden pavement with asphalt from Trinidad. Trinidad asphalt, Barber said, was "a cheap, desirable, smooth, clean, noiseless pavement, easy to repair and impermeable." Give him the contract, he said, and he would import and pave the streets of the nation's capital with Trinidad asphalt.

By the late 1870s and early 1880s, Barber, with Albright as his partner, had expanded operations to Baltimore, Boston, Erie, and Youngstown. The asphalt-paving business was too good to leave behind,

Massive railroad trestle built by Albright on Buffalo's waterfront, circa 1884.

Reproduction by permission of the Grosvenor Room, Buffalo &
Erie County Public Library, Buffalo, NY

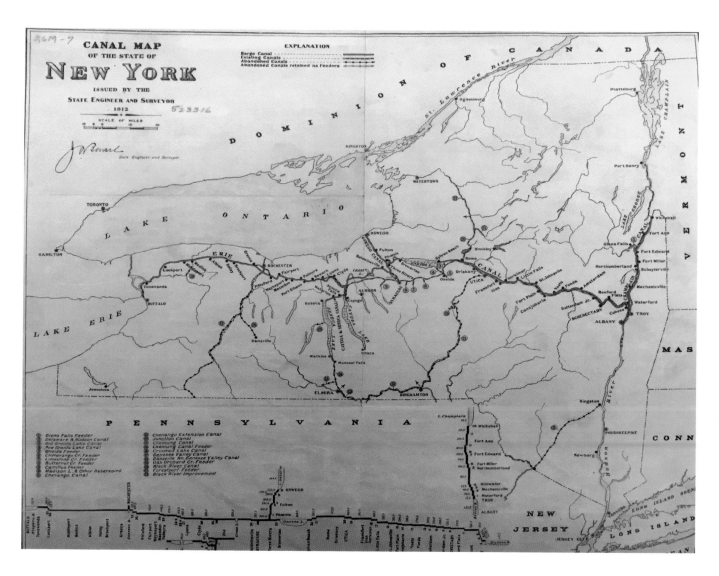

Although drawn in 1912, this map clearly illustrates the role that small, feeder canals played in the creation of the emerging national economy that enabled the rise of John J. Albright, Andrew Langdon and others in late 19th century Buffalo.

Reproduction by permission of the Grosvenor Room, Buffalo & Erie County Public Library, Buffalo, NY

THE RICHMOND ELEVATOR. (See opposite page.)

One of the many grain elevators that packed the waterfront during Albright's early years in Buffalo.

Reproduction by permission of the Grosvenor Room, Buffalo & Erie County Public Library, Buffalo, NY

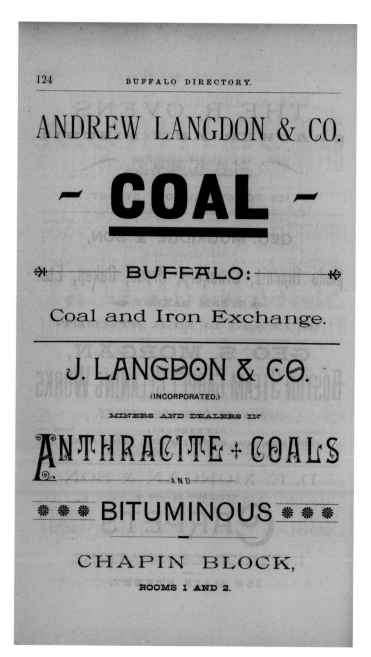

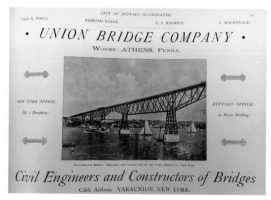

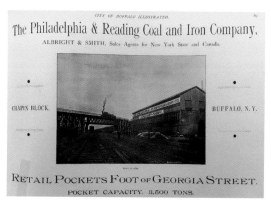

The Washington Market, also sometimes known as the Chippewa Market, was located on the square block bordered by Washington, Chippewa, and Ellicott streets. It was the largest retail market in Buffalo. The stalls within the large brick building were leased by butchers, and around the outside of the building were dozens of stalls where poultry, butter, fruits, and vegetables were sold. Wagons stood on the side of the streets where shoppers walked around among them, buying from them. Stalls in front of the market offered crockery, tins, knit goods, and all sorts of other useful products. Did Albright stop here in the evening on the way home from work when, it was said, "the market is lit by gas and many of the outside stands use torch lights, so that as one approached the market at night the scene is a brilliant and active one"? Or did he and Harriet come down to the market with their three children on Saturday, which, according to a contemporary account, "was the greatest market day, for upon that day from early morning till midnight the narrow pavements between the stalls are so crowded that even market-men and farmers can scarcely find room to move about"?[6]

Paving contract between Mayor Grover Cleveland and the Barber Asphalt Paving Company, signed by Amzi Barber and John J. Albright in 1882.

Courtesy of The Buffalo History Museum, used by permission

CHIPPEWA MARKET.

The Washington/Chippewa Market in the pre-automobile era, a part of Albright's daily landscape in turn-of-the-century Buffalo.

Reproduction by permission of the Grosvenor Room, Buffalo & Erie County Public Library, Buffalo, NY

The "new" downtown Buffalo, circa 1896. Whither the First
Presbyterian Church?

*Reproduction by permission of the Grosvenor Room, Buffalo & Erie
County Public Library, Buffalo, NY*

TOP: Downtown Buffalo as Albright would have seen it upon his return from his Grand Tour in 1890. This is a view across Main near Eagle Street, circa 1890.

Reproduction by permission of the Grosvenor Room, Buffalo & Erie County Public Library, Buffalo, NY

BOTTOM: We know from other photographs that Albright liked to ride a bicycle. Did he ever bike from his home on W. Ferry to his office in The Chapin Block at Main and Swan Street? A view of Main and Chippewa streets, circa 1890.

Reproduction by permission of the Grosvenor Room, Buffalo & Erie County Public Library, Buffalo, NY

Altman's, circa 1890. A few blocks from Albright's office, Altman's just might have been his haberdashery of choice.

Reproduction by permission of the Grosvenor Room, Buffalo & Erie County Public Library, Buffalo, NY

so when Albright moved to Buffalo he brought Barber Asphalt Paving with him. In 1882, he and Barber signed a contract with Buffalo Mayor Grover Cleveland, in which they agreed to pave what would be the first paved street in Buffalo: Bryant Street between Delaware Avenue and Main Street. Working out of their offices in the Chapin Block at Main and Swan, Barber Asphalt, with John J. Albright as CEO of the Buffalo branch, had by 1890 poured more than 2.8 million square yards of Trinidad asphalt, over "85% of all smooth pavements poured on the rapidly growing number of Buffalo streets."[4]

Albright had made a good choice. Buffalo fit him to a tee. Having spent the first five years of his residence in Buffalo in a home on Porter Avenue (next door to the Boarding School and Academy of the Holy Angels), in 1887 Albright bought a large estate on W. Ferry Street between Elmwood and Delaware that had been owned since midcentury by Charles Wadsworth. Later that year, John, Harriet, and their three children, Raymond, Ruth, and Langdon, moved into this large Gothic Revival style house with its tall, crenelated tower and deeply pitched roofs that Wadsworth had built in the 1850s. Over the next decade or so the Albrights increased the size of their property. In 1890, they bought the lot at the northeast corner of Elmwood Avenue and W. Ferry Street, which included a tennis court maintained by the Buffalo Tennis Club. In 1905, they bought Engine No. 5 from the city, the magnificent fire house on the Cleveland Avenue side of the property which serves today as a private home.[5]

It is tempting to contemplate what Albright's daily life in Buffalo, circa 1890, might have been like. How did he get to his office in the Chapin Block on Main and Swan streets? How much time did he spend in Frederick Law Olmsted's recently completed Delaware Park? Did he visit Assumption Parish and the booming Italian neighborhoods on the West and East Sides? Certainly, as we shall see, he was aware of the large Italian "colony" that was emerging on Seneca Street just a few blocks from his office on Main and Swan streets.

Did he shop at Altman Brothers, a large men's clothing store at Ellicott and Seneca streets owned by three brothers from Rochester, Issac, Jacob, and Henry, children of German Jewish immigrants who had been operating a store at this location since the late 1850s?[6] Did Albright buy his custom-made boots from Louis Goldstein next door? Did he ever ride on the Belt Line Railroad and visit the rapidly emerging Polish neighborhood in Black Rock? Or walk from his office on lower Main Street to the growing community of southern Italians that was emerging a few, short blocks away on Swan Street? Did he dine at the luminous Roof Garden, located on an entire square block at Main and High streets?[7]

Did Albright walk from his new home on W. Ferry to Norwood Avenue where, at the intersection of Norwood and Summer Street, stood Olympic Field, home to Buffalo's first professional baseball team, the Buffalo Bisons? Did he see the great Frank Grant, the first African-American baseball player ever to play in the majors, a switch-hitting right fielder who played for the Bisons between 1888 and 1890, lead the International League with a .344 batting average in 1889? And, we might also wonder, which one of Buffalo's many daily papers he read: *The Evening News?*

The Evening Times? The Express? The Commercial? The Advertiser?) Did he practice his German by reading the daily *Der Weltburger?* (Beginning around 1910 the Albrights had a German housekeeper referred to as "Soy" among whose duties was teaching the family to speak German.)

For a large number of those living in Buffalo during the late nineteenth century, the city had become a phenomenal source of wealth. Albright, with a seemingly Midas-like touch, quickly made a fortune. In 1888, Albright's grandson Birge reports, his grandfather, who sold his coal business to the Philadelphia and Reading Railroad for the staggering sum of $550,000 (more than $10 million in today's dollars) had "more than enough money for him to be able to retire and take his wife and three children to Europe and Egypt for fourteen months."[8] Leaving sometime in 1888-1889, the spectacular tour took the Albright family—John, Harriet, Raymond, Ruth, and Langdon—to France, Holland, Belgium, Switzerland, England, Italy, Greece, and Egypt. Beyond that, we know very little. Fortunately, Raymond, the Albright's thirteen-year-old son, took with him a brand new camera, the Kodak No. 1, recently developed by George Eastman and manufactured by the Eastman Dry Plate and Film Company in Rochester, New York.

Raymond started shooting the family trip immediately, capturing several powerful images of the roaring Atlantic Ocean from the deck of the steamer. He was intrepid, walking on deck in the midst of a storm and taking pictures of passengers steadying themselves against the wind. There are others, too, most notably a photograph, perhaps taken through a

LEFT: A photograph from a double-decker bus in an unidentified European city taken by Raymond K. Albright, an accomplished street photographer at the age of 14, during the Albright family's Grand Tour, 1888-1889.

Courtesy of George Eastman Museum

RIGHT: Hanging laundry at 730 W. Ferry, round image, probably taken by Raymond K. Albright with the Kodak 1, 1888.

Courtesy of George Eastman Museum

Kodak 1
National Media Museum

Conceived by George Eastman as a way to jettison cumbersome equipment and complicated technical maneuvers, the Kodak No. 1 required the would-be photographer to follow just three simple steps: "(1) Pull the string. (2) Turn the key. (3) Press the button." Despite its expense ($25 then, $650 today), the Kodak No. I sparked a national craze and in the process revolutionized photography. Housed in a light wooden box no more than four inches high and six inches deep, the camera, weighing less than two pounds, allowed anyone, even a young teenager like Raymond K. Albright, to become a photographer.

Raymond practiced with his new camera by taking pictures in and around the family's homestead on West Ferry Street. The first several dozen or so of the images, housed in the Collections Department at the George Eastman Museum, are wonderful snap-shots, not unlike Susan Albright Reed's memoir written a full century later, of the life and times of the home: there's a picture of the dining room table set for dinner; several views down a hall; a close up of the enormous fireplace. The most engaging of these practice shots are those taken outside including the Albrights' maids hanging up wet laundry to dry.

The Kodak No. 1 was not only portable and easy to operate but the roll of film inside the camera stored no fewer than one hundred images. When filled to capacity, the camera was sent back to Kodak in Rochester, where it was processed before being returned to the owner. Given the two-to-three hundred photographs that Raymond's widow gave to the Eastman House following his death in 1954, it is clear that this young and eager photographer took at least three of the Kodak Is with him.

TOP LEFT: Mr. and Mrs. Albright walking down Mount Vesuvius accompanied by guides. Photo by Raymond K. Albright, 1888-89.
Courtesy of George Eastman Museum

BOTTOM LEFT: "J.J.A. on Donkey." Note Raymond Albright's shadow in the lower right corner of the photograph.
Courtesy of George Eastman Museum

porthole, of another liner crossing the ocean in the opposite direction.

Raymond gained confidence once they landed in Europe. His collection at the Eastman House, perhaps the greatest repository anywhere of travel photographs taken by one photographer, contains many extraordinary images of street-scenes, churches, traffic, and people. Travelling south from the capitals of Western Europe, the Albright entourage—Mr. and Mrs. John J. and their three children—made their way to Greece. There, as is so clearly reflected in one of Raymond's close-up photos of the Acropolis in Athens, the idea was born that would inspire Albright and his architect, E. B. Green, as they conceived their plans for the Albright Art Gallery more than ten years later.

From Greece they travelled to Naples where they visited Mount Vesuvius. In one of the few photographs of his mother, Harriet Langdon, Raymond captures a clearly happy woman as she is carried first up and then down the steep hill leading to the top of the volcano.

Accompanied by two Albright descendants—great-grandson Rob Hawley and his daughter Liz, the great man's great-great-granddaughter—I pored through these hundreds of carefully stored images in the basement of the Eastman House. What is most noticeable, at least to me, is the utter absence of images of the man himself, the father of our young photographer. Given what we have since learned about his lifelong quest for privacy, even anonymity, Albright, we can guess, stayed clear of his son's camera, refusing to be "shot" by anyone, let alone his son. But then, searching through a cache of photos taken in Egypt, there, amidst the temples, the hieroglyphs, and the pyramids, was finally a photograph taken by Raymond of his father, captioned simply "JJ on donkey El Kabob."

THREE

Towards the New Century

Fully restored and seemingly rejuvenated by his long voyage (after all, Albright was a mere forty years old when he embarked), Albright picked up where he had left off following his return to Buffalo in early 1890. Prior to his departure, Albright had made three decisions that would influence both his future and the future of his recently adopted city: he joined the First Presbyterian Church, becoming acquainted there with architect Edward B. Green; he became a director of the Buffalo Fine Arts Academy; and three years before Joseph Schoellkopf rescued a failing Niagara Falls company and, out of the ruins of that failure, created what would become the Niagara Falls Power Company, John J. Albright founded and incorporated the Ontario Power Company. Located on the Canadian side of the Niagara River, the OPC, it was noted, was to "supply manufacturers, corporations, and persons with water, hydraulic, electric, or other power."[1] All of this work and more would, thanks to the close relationship that Albright had developed with a young architect named Edward Broadbent Green, come to fruition during the 1890s.

E. B. Green played a major role in the life and work of John J. Albright, and their relationship is one of enormous significance for the city of Buffalo. He was born in Utica, New York, in 1855 and moved to Buffalo in 1881, at or about the same time as Albright.

While Green designed two private homes and the crematory adjacent to Forest Lawn Cemetery in the mid-1880s, he received his first significant commission in 1889, when he was hired to design a new building for the First Presbyterian Church, the oldest church in Buffalo. It was to be located on a plot of land that is today known as Symphony Circle.

Ever since its founding in 1812, the First Presbyterian Church had been housed in a wood-frame building and later in an imposing brick one at the corner of Main and Church streets. That building, "the Brick Church," was a much-loved red-brick structure trimmed in white with a balustrade circling the roof. Mounted above a large clock visible from afar was a bell tower with a six-sided golden dome that, when it blazed in the sunlight, served as a landmark for Lake Erie mariners. By the mid-1880s, however, the once bucolic intersection of Main and Church had become increasingly busy, surrounded by a noisy and fast-growing downtown business district. In 1889, following a contentious and deeply divisive struggle among its congregation, a decision was reached to move, and E. B. Green was awarded the commission to design a new church. While we do not know what role Albright, a member of the church since 1887, played in the choice of Green, it is safe to say that he was influential. Indeed, upon returning from his world

FIRST PRESBYTERIAN CHURCH, BUFFALO, N. Y.
Dedicated 1827.

LEFT: Welcome House. Founded by Harriet Langdon Albright and others from the First Presbyterian Church, Welcome House was modeled after Hull House in Chicago and was located in the heart of a growing Italian and Syrian neighborhood on and around Seneca Street. Designed by E.B. Green and completed in 1894.

Reproduction by permission of the Grosvenor Room, Buffalo & Erie County Public Library, Buffalo, NY

RIGHT: First Presbyterian Church, known as "the Brick Church," at the corner of Main and Church streets, prior to the construction of the Erie County Savings Bank.

Reproduction by permission of the Grosvenor Room, Buffalo & Erie County Public Library, Buffalo, NY

tour in 1891, Albright chose Green to design a public library in Scranton, Pennsylvania. As was his wont, Green turned to Europe for inspiration, this time to the Cluny Museum in Paris as a model for the library. Built in honor of his parents on the site of the Albright homestead, the Albright Memorial Library, completed in 1893, is a Scranton treasure, its architectural excellence recognized by its listing on the National Register of Historic Places.

The Albright Memorial Library sealed the relationship with Green. Within a few years, the Women's Circle at First Presbyterian, of which Harriet Albright was a member, became concerned with the growing evidence of poverty in a city that was struggling to deal with the challenge not only of increased immigration but the Crash of 1893, as well. In 1894, the Women's Circle hired E. B. Green to design a settlement house for the church on Seneca Street in a particularly hard-hit neighborhood. While the building was undergoing construction, the Circle hired one of the leading social workers in the nation, Mary Remington from New Haven, Connecticut, a disciple of Jane Addams, the pioneer American activist/social reformer. Working out of temporary quarters at Seneca and Michigan Streets and with the moral support of the Women's Circle and the financial support of John J. Albright, Remington created a Sunday school, a commissary, and a kindergarten for the growing numbers of primarily Italian families who now lived in the city. In addition, Albright bought a 5000-square-foot lot adjacent to the planned building for the creation of what one newspaper described as "a superb playground for the summer, something many of the children in the neighborhood have never had before. In the afternoon the gates are opened and all the children in the neighborhood who wish to come are free to take advantage of the pleasures of Mr. Albright's playground."[2] In January 1898, Welcome House, designed by Green in a style that Green scholar Catherine Faust says resembled "an English Medieval Guildhall," opened to an ecstatic reception in that distressed part of town.[3]

In 1895, Albright's wife, Harriet, died. Although they had been married for twenty-three years, Harriet, at least as far as I can tell, left not a trace. Indeed, with the exception of the few photographs taken by her son Raymond during their 1888 Grand Tour, Harriet seems to be missing from the historical record. Despite that absence, her husband, John, seems to have cherished her memory. In 1902, when John C. Olmsted, Frederick Law Olmsted's son, was working on the grounds of the Albright's Ferry Street estate, he found the property "thick with plantings, trees, etc." and suggested that "quite a bit of thinning would be desirable." Albright, Olmsted contended, "was much averse to changing anything associated with things as they were during the life of his first wife." Albright's gardener confirmed his employer's attachment to the memory of his wife, telling Olmsted, "Nothing would induce Mr. Albright to cut down any of the old apple or fruit trees."[4] Upon Harriet's death, Albright inquired of Smith College whether they knew of a recent graduate who might prove to be a suitable companion for his teenaged daughter, Ruth. Later that year Susan Fuller, who her grandson Birge described as "a young lady of Shaker stock from Lancaster, Massachusetts," arrived. Two years later, in 1897, John J. Albright and Susan Fuller were married.

Exterior of the Albright home at 730 W. Ferry Street. Winter scene.

Courtesy of The Buffalo History Museum, used by permission

In 1901, we know not when or how, John and Susan Albright's striking Gothic home, the one that they'd been living in since the late 1880s, burned to the ground. The impact on the family, though unrecorded, must have been devastating. Imagine the loss not only of paintings and furniture, of priceless woodwork and fantastic finishes, but what might just have been the treasure trove of letters and diaries and photographs and records that I have sought so diligently to find. Literally "burned" badly by the certain trauma of this incredible loss, perhaps Albright swore never again to record a thought, to save a record, or to preserve a memory.

Lost from the record too is the family's response to this undoubtedly horrific event. Where was the family when the fire occurred? Did any of them rush back into the conflagration to save their treasured belongings? How is it that Raymond's photographs survived while all else seems to have gone up in flames? And where did the Albrights live after the fire, during the four years while they waited for Edward B. Green to complete their new home?

To rebuild, Albright called on Edward B. Green. Green's assignment, to design and build what would become one of the most glorious homes in a city filled with them, was prodigious. Whether it was his or his patron's idea is not known (there are no images of the place in Raymond's collection of travel photographs), within a year there began to appear on the square-block of land located between Elmwood and Delaware avenues, Ferry and Cleveland streets, a perfect replica of one of the great English country manors, St. Catherine's Court. Located in the middle

Exterior of the Albright home on W. Ferry Street between Elmwood and Delaware Avenue. Built in circa 1850, Albright's first home on W. Ferry Street burned in circa 1900.

Courtesy of The Buffalo History Museum, used by permission

TOP: Note the square block between Elmwood and Delaware, Ferry and Cleveland, the bulk of which, in this 1902 map, was covered by the Albright Estate.

Courtesy of the Buffalo History Museum, used by permission

BOTTOM: When it was completed in 1896, the Ellicott Square Building became the largest office building in the world.

Courtesy of the Buffalo History Museum, used by permission

of the grounds so meticulously designed by the Olmstead firm, was a large complex of buildings. There was a Tudor-style stable; a group of buildings facing Cleveland Avenue that included a chauffeur's apartment and a gardener's house; a long drive that led up to the home; a tennis court, three greenhouses, and a chicken house. Surrounding the house itself were sloping lawns with many different varieties of trees, shrubs, flowers, and vegetable gardens. Inside the home was a large two-story octagonal entrance hall, a lofty music room, and a "flower room" with a marble floor and Greek columns. Green's relationship with Albright was both personal and professional and, as we shall see, had only just begun.[5]

The landscape of Albright's Buffalo was changing drastically all around him, particularly downtown. Fueled by the electric streetcar and the first use of structural steel as a building material, a new, dynamic downtown was emerging—a central business district that, by the turn-of-the century, had become the business, retail, and entertainment center for the entire region. Riding on a newly electrified rapid transit system, the people of Buffalo, for so long isolated in ancestral ethnic neighborhoods, were able to travel downtown. Retail business boomed as large new department stores—the largest, Hengerer's, opened in 1904—were built to accommodate the flood. Hotels and restaurants, music halls, and theaters all sought downtown locations as the social and cultural center of the city shifted away from Buffalo's neighborhoods to Buffalo's new and bustling downtown. The church steeple, so long the symbolic icon of downtown Buffalo, was being replaced by theater marquees and

corporate towers. The First Presbyterian Church was demolished, replaced by the gigantic Erie County Savings Bank. A row of small, wooden buildings at Church and Pearl streets was cleared for the sleek Adler-Sullivan-designed Guaranty Building. The North Presbyterian Church on Main and Huron was demolished and replaced by the Hippodrome Theater, while the Central Presbyterian Church on Pearl and Genesee streets gave way to the Majestic Theater.

No building better symbolized the "New Buffalo" than the Ellicott Square Building, where John J. Albright maintained an office at the turn-of-the-century. When it was completed in 1896 the ten-story, full-square-block building was, with 800 separate offices, the largest office building in the world. The Ellicott Square Building was a marvel of mixed-use, a dynamic, exciting, and intensely theatrical hub of activity where everything, including both Russian and Turkish baths, was available. In the Ellicott Square Building there were several firsts. Hotelier Eldridge Statler's first restaurant was located there and was, some say, the first "cafeteria" ever. And although some dispute this, the first purpose-built movie theater in the world was opened there by Mitchell and Moe Mark in the basement of the building. Called both "Edisonia Hall" and "Vitascope Hall," the theater was, the Mark brothers said, "fitted up as a suitable place for the proper display of the marvelous possibilities of Edison's wonder worker—the perfected Vitascope." Did Albright have his lunch at Statler's Restaurant? Did he go underground to the Vitascope to watch some of the first newsreels ever shown anywhere: *The Watermelon Contest, The Coronation of Tsar Nicholas II,* or the Lumiere Brothers' film of the intersection of Broadway and Union Square in New York City?[6]

Around the time Albright returned from his European grand tour in 1890 he became increasingly concerned about the education of his two sons, Raymond, now fifteen years old, and Langdon, ten, and gave serious thought and considerable attention to creating for them what he considered to be a proper school. Although the Buffalo Female Academy had been educating the daughters of Buffalo's elite since the middle of the century, there was no equivalent school for the young men of the city. Unlike others of his social class, Albright did not want his children to go away for school and, beginning in 1891 he along with some of his closest associates—the lumber titan William Gratwick among them—initiated a planning process that would, one year later, lead to the creation of The Nichols School, named for William Nichols, the school's first headmaster.

Nichols, who was brought to the attention of Albright and the others by Charles Eliot, the esteemed president of Harvard University, was a dyed-in-the-wool New Englander with deeply traditional educational views. While Eliot himself was an advocate for a more progressive educational agenda, he recommended Nichols, he said, because he was, as John Sessions, Nichols School's historian and long-term faculty member describes, "a successful teacher of high character and aims and has wide experiences with all sorts of boys."[7] Other recommendations stressed Nichols' efficiency. "His success," said one referent, "was due to his great efficiency." Another called Nichols "one of the most efficient teachers engaged in preparing boys for college." He was, in addition, a traditionalist, "a parent and an educator of the old-fashioned New England type with very little leniency in his disposition." These traits attracted the attention of Albright, Gratwick, and others, and in June 1892 Nichols was hired. "Mr. William Nichols," an article in a local paper reported, "will open a school in Buffalo in which boys will be fitted for the leading colleges and technical schools."[8]

Housed in a Tudor-style wood-frame building at 35 Norwood Avenue, which, according to Sessions, was financed by Albright, the new Nichols School opened in the fall of 1892 with three faculty members and approximately twenty students. With a narrow curriculum based on Nichols' New England training rooted in the teaching of Greek and Latin and science and math (neither art nor history were offered), the school struggled through the last years of the old century and into the first years of the new.

Times were tough and even before Nichols died in 1907, Albright "must have known that the school was in trouble."[9] Concerned for his community as well as for the welfare of his two sons from his second marriage, Albright came to the rescue, offering the $25,000 needed to build the kind of school that incorporated demanding educational goals. An "important announcement," made public in the summer of 1908, outlined the ideas for the school. Sessions suggests that this document was strongly influenced by Albright; it "proposed little less than a remaking of the school in terms of both educational philosophy and bricks and mortar."

According to Sessions, the most striking change (one that he says Albright encouraged) was the lengthening of

Albright Hall, The Nichols School.

Reproduction by permission of the Grosvenor Room, Buffalo & Erie County Public Library, Buffalo, NY

the school day. As one deeply knowledgeable about the school, Sessions says this change "provided the opportunity to improve the educational, athletic, and moral dimensions of the school." Now, Sessions wrote, there would be far more opportunity for "increased contact between the students and their teachers." And, equally significant, "The extra time would permit the sports program to be greatly expanded. Proper practices could be organized on proper fields and in a proper gymnasium, and new sports, like hockey, could be offered." [10]

In September 1909, The Nichols School opened on a new campus (bought largely with funds guaranteed by John Albright and his oldest son, Raymond) and housed in a new building designed by Albright's friend and architect, E. B. Green. Armed with a brand new lease on life, the new school for boys entered a new era. Well over one hundred years later, The Nichols School remains a jewel in the crown of Buffalo's educational institutions, rooted on a foundation created largely as a result of the vision of John J. Albright.

FOUR

Phantasmagoric Kingdoms

As the nineteenth century came to a close, two momentous events occurred which, for better or for worse, determined the destiny and the character of the city of Buffalo for the duration of the next century: one was the opening of the Lackawanna Steel Company; the other, the mounting of the Pan-American Exposition. It is staggering to consider that at the same time, in the same city, in places separated by only a few miles, two whole new and different realities existed, one a mammoth, Piranesi-like hulking industrial complex, the other a spectacular, fantasy-filled world's fair. One would vanish after one year, the other after eighty. The role played by John J. Albright in these events, though largely undocumented, appears to have been essential; most notably regarding the Lackawanna Iron and Steel Company in 1900.

The much-heralded arrival of Lackawanna Steel and its devastating departure barely eighty years later frame, as perhaps no other events do, the triumph and the tragedy, the power and the pathos that is the complicated history of industry in America. Although others were involved, there was no one more influential in its unfolding than John J. Albright.

The Albrights, father Joseph Jacob and son John Joseph, had deep roots in the early origins of what would become the American steel industry. Joseph Jacob had come of age in Scranton with the Scranton family, connected through business and marriage. This relationship continued throughout the last quarter of the nineteenth century when a conversation started between these two families that led to a partnership that forever altered the history of Buffalo.

Regardless of how their conversation started—did Walter Scranton and John J. Albright talk on the phone? Did they travel by train, a round trip of about sixteen hours? Did Scranton come to Buffalo? Did Albright go to Scranton? Perhaps they met at Jekyll Island, the exclusive island resort off the coast of Georgia where Albright had wintered since the late 1880s. Or perhaps they both travelled to Wilmurt, the remote New York lakefront community where Albright passed his summers in a chalet designed by his favorite architect, E. B. Green. Scranton and Albright were birds of a feather, drawn to each other by family, business ties, and a common world view. Both men were modernists, fettered by neither tradition nor sentiment. They were impelled by disposition as well as the culture of the world they lived in to seek new and creative solutions—most often driven by their knowledge of engineering—to the challenges they faced. Together, they sought and created a partnership that would transform the world in which they lived.

Their future, they had come to know, was in Buffalo. For Scranton, a new plant in Buffalo offered proximity

THE TRANSFORMATION OF STONY POINT: AMONG THE STEEL WORKS' FURNACES AND CHIMNEYS.
View from the Lake, off the Stony Point breakwater.—Drawn by H. H. Green.

Lackawanna Steel in the news, from the Scrapbook Collection. Above: A fantastical realization, part photo, part drawing, of Lackawanna Steel, circa 1902.

Reproduction by permission of the Grosvenor Room, Buffalo & Erie County Public Library, Buffalo, NY

to two natural resources essential for the production of steel: iron from the Mesabi range in Minnesota and electrical power from Niagara Falls. Buffalo would bring him close to these and, he hoped, far from the rapidly spreading seeds of discontent being sown by the United Mine Workers throughout the coalfields and iron plants of central Pennsylvania. Scranton and Lackawanna Steel was a big catch. Albright and a small coterie of fellow industrialists did everything they could to lure Scranton's company to Buffalo.

Although the courtship had begun months before, it culminated at a highly celebrated luncheon described in many chronicles of turn-of-the-century Buffalo held at the Delaware Avenue home of John Milburn, Buffalo's preeminent corporate attorney and "rainmaker." There, over the Fourth of July weekend of 1899, Scranton was wined and dined by the city's leading industrialists, Albright prominent among them. In the compelling language of an accomplished attorney, Milburn wooed Scranton. Buffalo, he declared, possessed all the necessary ingredients and conditions for the creation of a new economy rooted firmly in industry. It was the perfect location at which to build the new plant: abundant natural resources were available in the form of raw iron, as well as an endless supply of electrical power generated by the falls of Niagara. A steady stream of immigrant-laborers was arriving daily from Central and Eastern Europe. And an ample supply of capital would be provided, as we shall see, by the soon-to-be-reinvented Marine National Bank.

By the end of 1899, the deal was done, the result of much touted but immediately controversial negotiations. Were the low prices that Albright negotiated for these acres of valuable lakefront land just south of Buffalo the result of, as some thought, a deception? Did Albright, as some of his critics hinted, represent that the land he was purchasing would be used, not for the steel plant, but rather as the site of the Pan-American Exposition? Or, as others said, for Frederick Law Olmsted's new park in South Buffalo? How many actually knew that John Albright was acquiring land for his Stony Point Land Company on which would soon be built the Lackawanna Steel Company?

Regardless of how these deals were accomplished or the motives involved, the land was assembled and the necessary capital was raised: three of the four million dollars that Scranton had insisted on at Milburn's Fourth of July luncheon. How it happened and who arranged it we do not know, but the "Vanderbilt interests in New York City" came up with the balance "to conserve the interests of the New York Central Railroad" according to their lawyers.[1]

Although completed in outline, the move of Lackawanna Steel to Buffalo had yet to be officially announced. In an effort to seek some confirmation of the growing rumors that a move to Buffalo by the Lackawanna Steel Company was imminent, in December 1899 a reporter for the *Buffalo Evening News* was able to accomplish what no one else had been able to: pin down John Albright for an interview. Albright was unaccustomed to speaking with the press, and his impatience with the persistent questioning is obvious in the testy answers that he offered.

Pressed as to the accuracy of the circulating reports, Albright said: "I don't know what I can say beyond

—Photo by The Sunday Courier's Staff Photographer, Oscar A. Simon.

At the Biggest of Steel Plants—When the Day's Work Is Done the Thousands of Toilers Hurry Towards the Gates.

Days end at Lackawanna Steel, circa 1902. (Who is Oscar A. Simon, the photographer who took this extraordinary photograph?)

Reproduction by permission of the Grosvenor Room, Buffalo & Erie County Public Library, Buffalo, NY

what has been said in the way of giving assurance that the steel plant certainly will be built at Buffalo." Unwilling to leave well enough alone, the reporter persisted, trying to push Albright to make a more definitive statement: "But will anything of a tangible nature be done in the near future?" he asked. With this question, Albright, in the patronizing, lèse-majesté way that Gilded Age robber barons treated the press and the public, replied:

It seems strange to me that the people seem unable to understand that a work of this magnitude cannot be done in a week or a month. It is not a plant that can be constructed under a temporary shed. Imagine the miles of plans that must be made. Think of the great stretch of machinery that must be planned for and the drawings that must be made. Why, if all the mechanical engineers and draftsmen in the country were employed upon this work it could not be done in a week as many people seem to think. The work is progressing as rapidly as possible.

When asked when the work on the plant would begin, Albright refused to budge, suggesting that the topic was off-limits to the press: "I cannot go into details. There are naturally many things in such an enterprise as that which cannot be talked about in the newspapers." When asked if the delay, by preventing the company from taking advantage of the then high price of iron and steel, was not hurting the company, Albright could not resist: "The company that is back of this enterprise is not building this plant because of the present advance in the price of steel and iron. They are building for the years that are to come. They are

building a great plant that will be one of the permanent concerns of the country." Certainly, the reporter assumed, Albright could at least confirm that the plan was in the works and that the move from Scranton to Buffalo was a certainty? Again, Albright stonewalled, citing the dangers of an overly inquisitive press that, at least in Albright's mind, bordered on the irresponsible:

That is one of the things I cannot talk about. But it seems to me that the fact that a million and a half of dollars have been expended here preparatory to building the big steel plant ought to be sufficient assurance to the people that the work will be completed. I regret very much that so much nonsense has been printed in some of the papers about the Rockefellers and other things in connection with this enterprise. It does nobody any good and it injures Buffalo on the outside.[2]

The end of 1900 saw not one but two new, enormous communities—phantasmagorical landscapes—being born in Buffalo. The home of Lackawanna Steel, the nation's second largest steel plant, was slowly and methodically being erected on the shores of Lake Erie in what would soon become the city of Lackawanna. Just a few miles away on the edges of Delaware Park, a whole other kind of new community, equally mesmerizing, was being built: the Pan-American Exposition. The exposition would come to exert, in ways that are perhaps more perplexing and challenging to define, an influence on twentieth century Buffalo equal to the colossus that was the Lackawanna Iron and Steel Company. Both owed much to the leadership of John J. Albright.

Although Albright was a member of the exposition's board of directors, none of the sources dealing with the Pan-Am describe his role with any degree of specificity. While some of the board meetings may well have occurred at his offices in the Ellicott Square Building, the absence of minutes of those meetings or any correspondence from Albright to his fellow board members leaves us guessing. Given his interests, it is likely that he had a say in deciding upon many of the exposition's buildings—one each for agriculture, manufacturing, electricity, machinery, transportation, mining, and forestry. Although the electrical power transmission capabilities that Albright would develop a few years later were not yet up and running, he certainly would as well have had a hand in creating the Electric Tower, the iconic centerpiece of the whole exposition. It is easy to imagine Albright, standing with John Milburn on the porch of the latter's home at Delaware and Ferry, just around the corner from Albright's home, watching the extraordinary spectacle of light that captured the attention and stimulated the imagination of the tens of thousands of people who came to the Pan-American Exposition. The Electric Tower was the exposition's most popular attraction, extensively described in the many quasi-magical press accounts of the day:

> *The Tower is a great center of brilliancy with the appearance of a whole city in illumination. There are perhaps not a half million electric bulbs, but there are hundreds and thousands of them and you are willing to believe that there might be millions. It shines like diamonds, a transparent soft structure of sunlight. There it stands, glowing with the light of many thousands of bulbs flashing its image in the basin at its feet, showing its gleaming dome to the people in neighboring cities. Its beauty is transcendent.* [3]

Can we not safely assume, given his interest in and knowledge of electricity, that John J. Albright was the genius behind this awesome structure?

Still, we don't know if the Albrights ever visited the exposition. Did John and his new wife, Susan Fuller Albright, wheel their three children—three-year-old John J. Jr., two-year-old Elizabeth, and one-year-old Fuller—in baby carriages around the Midway? What might Albright, the stern, visionary engineer, have thought of what he would have seen there? Did they visit the "Old Plantation," where visitors were assured that "the negroes were selected from the best class of southern darkies, for Skip Dandy, the concessionaire, has the reputation of not tolerating anything shiftless or degrading about him." [4] Were they aware of Mary Talbert's efforts to mount instead an exhibition that documented the achievements of African Americans in industry, literature, and journalism since the Emancipation Proclamation? What did they think about "The Streets of Mexico"? Did they ride "The Trip to the Moon" and the Aeriocycle, a relative of the recently invented Ferris Wheel, from which, at night, after dark, the view of the illuminated fairgrounds was the best? Is it the Albright family we see in that photograph, sitting at a picnic bench in the large outdoor beer garden at Alt Nuremberg, dining on the house specialty, wienerwurst and German fried potatoes? Perhaps. But it also well may not be, for had they gone, would not

Susan, an avid photographer, have brought along her omnipresent camera and taken pictures of her own?

And where was John Albright on that fateful day in September 1901, when the president of the United States, William McKinley, was shot? What were his thoughts on the assassination and on the death of McKinley a week later at John Milburn's home on Delaware Avenue, just around the corner from the Albrights' Ferry Street home? Did he harbor fears that perhaps he, like McKinley and King Umberto of Italy just the year before, would be the target of an anarchist's bullet? Indeed, what were his actions in the days that followed? On September 14, 1901, was he present at the inauguration of Theodore Roosevelt as president of the United States at the home of Ansley Wilcox, an influential attorney whom Albright most certainly knew? Was he anywhere near the exposition grounds when, on "Buffalo Day," November 1, the exposition's last day, a rowdy crowd rampaged the grounds?

> *People went mad. They were seized with the desire to destroy. Depredation and destruction were carried on in the boldest manner all along the Midway. Electric lights were jerked from their posts and thousands of them were smashed to the ground. Windows were shattered and doors were kicked down and policemen were pushed aside as if they were stuffed ornaments. The National Glass Exhibit was completely destroyed. Pabst's Café was demolished, and Cleopatra's needle was torn to the ground.*[5]

Was he there? He certainly knew about these events. Everybody did. But about his thoughts and feelings, we know nothing.

In early December 1901, what remained of the exposition buildings was sold to the Harris Wrecking Company of Chicago. A local committee was formed to buy and preserve the Electric Tower as a lasting monument to the exposition. But with no apparent support from Albright, the committee failed to raise the necessary funds. On January 20, 1902, the statue of the Goddess of Light was sold to the Humphrey Popcorn Company of Cleveland, and the Electric Tower was finally demolished.[6]

While the one magical city was being dismantled, the gigantic complex of factories being built by the Lackawanna Iron and Steel Company was nearing completion. By 1904, the company had already built six open-hearth furnaces that would soon be producing light rails, steel plate, and steel slabs. In addition, miles of railroad track had been laid, some linking the plant directly to the coal regions of western Pennsylvania and others directly to the national railroad distribution network. Built, too, was a giant new ship canal intended exclusively for the use of massive lake boats bringing iron ore to Lackawanna's plant. Known as the "Union Ship Canal," it has in our day been dredged and cleaned and, in an interesting commentary on the fate of the infrastructure of this area's industrial economy, now functions as one of the region's most popular kayaking destinations. According to the website of the Erie County Industrial Development Agency, in addition to kayaking, the canal has become a place which "will provide ample shelter for juvenile lake fish species as well as anchors for native sea plants."

By 1904, Lackawanna Iron and Steel had taken millions of dollars of orders. While their primary

The Electric Tower. Did Albright, who would soon dominate the electric power industry at Niagara Falls, conceive of this iconic structure at the Pan-American Exposition?

Reproduction by permission of the Grosvenor Room, Buffalo & Erie County Public Library, Buffalo, NY

LEFT: The popular German restaurant on The Midway at the Pan-American Exposition. Any sightings of the Albright family?

Reproduction by permission of the Grosvenor Room, Buffalo & Erie County Public Library, Buffalo, NY

RIGHT: The Plantation, a controversial exhibit on the Midway.

Reproduction by permission of the Grosvenor Room, Buffalo & Erie County Public Library, Buffalo, NY

SMELTER AND MILL
Getting Copper
Ready for Use

IN A COPPER ROLLING MILL: SETTING UP NEW MILL.

IN A COPPER SMELTER: POURING THE WHITE HOT METAL TO MAKE BILLETS.—The pictures are from photographs by George J. Hare.

The newspapers were fascinated with the details of life and labor at the new steel plant and sent staff photographers there to cover it.

Reproduction by permission of the Grosvenor Room, Buffalo & Erie County Public Library, Buffalo, NY

customers were American railroads, they also sold rails to the Philippines, Australia, and Japan. In June 1906, Lieutenant Commander Shiegetoshi Takehucki visited the plant, accompanied perhaps by John J. Albright, and placed a multimillion dollar order for armor plating. By the end of 1904, Lackawanna had similar orders from Russia, Germany, and England.[7] As an engineer, a capitalist, and the person most responsible for the move of the Lackawanna company to Buffalo, John Albright's hands were surely engaged in all of this work, but how and to what degree, we do not know.

Meanwhile, the Lackawanna company faced the challenges of a topsy-turvy economy, one that with very little warning could slip out of control. This had happened in the 1870s and again in the 1890s. Then, in the early twentieth century, just as the company entered full production, the "Panic of 1907" wreaked havoc with the American economy. Within one year, steel production, which had reached more than one million tons in 1906, dropped by almost half. Layoffs followed and, by the end of 1907, fewer than two thousand of the six-thousand-man work force remained. The salaries of mill hands and office workers were cut by ten percent, the executive force was trimmed, and the long-time president of the company, Walter Scranton, the man who had worked with John Albright to bring Lackawanna Steel to Buffalo, was let go. The local press, which had been such eager supporters of the project, reporting in great detail virtually every aspect of the progress that the company had been making, began to sour. One paper, the usually bullish *Commercial Advertiser*, wrote in 1908: "There is no warrant for published statements intimating that the steel business is picking up again."[8]

At the Biggest of Steel Plants—One of the Great Cranes Picks Up a Locomotive and Poses for a Photograph.

The photographers were mesmerized by the phantasmagoric machinery.

Reproduction by permission of the Grosvenor Room, Buffalo & Erie County Public Library, Buffalo, NY

Suddenly, the press began to focus its attention on what was going wrong at Lackawanna, writing in gruesome detail about the accidents that seemed to be occurring on a daily basis: One, Julius Kolas, hit by a falling piece of ore, "was taken to the Emergency Hospital where it was found that both his hips were smashed, his right arm fractured, and that he had internal injuries. He died on the operating table." Another, August Pfohl, "was severally and perhaps fatally burned … He is resting at home as easily as can be expected and it is thought that he will be able to return to work. His legs, however, will be useless." [9]

What were Albright's thoughts and feelings? Where was his vaunted philanthropy, the generosity that had led him to build a settlement house, a school, and two extraordinary eponymous institutions: a library in Scranton and an art gallery in Buffalo? Where was the "Albright Wing" at the Lackawanna Emergency Hospital? The "Albright Water Treatment Plant" that might have mitigated the pollution of the new town's drinking water? Or the "Albright Playground" for the children trapped in the hellish environment that the Lackawanna Steel Company had created? Was he pleased with what his energy, vision, intelligence, and resources had wrought? Or disappointed? Did he sense, in the deepest regions of his intellect, that the magical setting at the Pan-Am that he helped to create was merely an ephemeral development that would, within a year, be sold and its remains carted off by a Chicago wrecking company? And that the Lackawanna Iron and Steel Company, acquired by Bethlehem Steel in 1923, within the course of a lifespan, would become, like the Pan-Am, shuttered, demolished, and barely mourned by a community in which so many people felt that they'd been had?

FIVE

Creating a Modern Banking System

What we do know is that Albright was seriously concerned about the ever-present instability and volatility of the turn-of-the-century American industrial economy. Despite the stolid appearances its titans projected—the shiny black top hats; the polished four-in-hands with their snappy-looking coachmen; starched chamber maids; and plumed, corpulent wives—the lives of the industrial leaders of the early twentieth century were filled with anxiety and financial uncertainty. Threatened by a culture that valued competition and feared regulation, that created a plethora of supply and a dearth of demand, the whole foundation of the American economy stood on shaky ground, subject to traumatic downturns in the business cycle on a regular basis. Desperately eager to bring stability to a vulnerable system, Albright and the small group of businessmen that were his colleagues did what they could to strengthen one of the most critical links in the economic chain: banking.

Given Albright's industrial appetites, he and his peers required ready access to large amounts of capital which was, in those days before the Federal Reserve Board, often not available. It was perhaps this effort that led him and a small group of other investors to form the Fidelity Trust and Guaranty Company of Buffalo in 1893. Albright's purpose in founding a trust company was, in addition to offering the usual trust and commercial banking functions, to act as a "bankers' bank" that would hold the reserves of other banks and institutions. One of Fidelity's customers, for example, was the Pan-American Exposition Company, whose bonds it held. In the panic that ensued following the death of President McKinley in September 1901, depositors concerned that the uncertainty of the exposition would negatively impact the fortunes of Fidelity began a run on the bank.

In the skittish world of banking and finance where rumors spread at the speed of light, the story of the "run" on the Fidelity made it into the *New York Times*. The *Times* reported that "a long line of anxious depositors reaching from the tellers' windows into the street stood for hours waiting to withdraw their money."[1] Albright's bank, however, though only eight years old, stood on a firm foundation. The rumors were unfounded. When two local banks offered funds—$250,000 from the Erie County Savings Bank, $100,000 from the Marine Bank—Fidelity's president, George V. Forman, one of the bank's founding partners along with Albright, politely demurred, "informing the two banks that the Fidelity Company needed no assistance."[2]

Despite his known role in formation of the Fidelity, no documentation other than a routine listing of officers in year-end reports, suggests the role that Albright might have played in the creation in 1893 of this

The Fidelity Trust Company was founded by Albright and others in 1900. This building, located at the northwest corner of Main and Swan streets, was designed for Albright by E.B. Green and completed in 1909. Undoubtedly inspired by Green's Albright Gallery, the Manufacturers and Traders Trust built their Neo-Classical structure across Swan Street in 1915. Photo circa 1920.

Reproduction by permission of the Grosvenor Room, Buffalo & Erie County Public Library, Buffalo, NY

Rogers, like his co-directors at the Marine, embodies the extent to which the creation of what was then referred to as "the new Buffalo" was rooted in a network of overlapping and interconnected relationships between bankers and industrialists. Born in central New York in 1851, Rogers moved to Buffalo in 1890, when he, like Albright who had moved here eight years earlier, was in his late thirties. By the end of that decade, Rogers, as much as Albright, had become a major player in the rapid transformations occurring in the local economy. According to accounts in the *Buffalo Evening News* several years later, it was Rogers who, working with Albright in 1899, had chosen the lakefront south of Buffalo for the new location of what would become Lackawanna Steel.[4] Along with Albright and Albright's closest colleague, Edmund B. Hayes, Rogers also led the subscription drive that raised the two million dollars required for the move. And it was he who, three years later, organized a little-known but highly significant trip to Chicago that led to the creation of yet another steel company, Buffalo and Susquehanna Steel. A contemporary account described the trip:

J. J. Albright, Edmund Hayes, and S. M. Clement have been interested in the plant for several years, though they had never seen the property. Mr. Rogers accordingly invited these men to accompany him on one of his periodic visits. Mr. Frank and Charles Goodyear (partners in the Goodyear Lumber and the Buffalo and Susquehanna Railroad), hearing of the proposed trip, tendered the use of his private railroad car for the occasion.[5]

While Albright seemed only to have gone along for the ride, the Goodyear brothers made the most of the journey. They were, the report continues, "so impressed with the capacity of the steel plant to produce tonnage for a railroad that they wished one established on the line of their own Buffalo and Susquehanna Railroad." It was a done deal. "The result of the trip was that Mr. Rogers and the Goodyear brothers joined forces to create the institution which, out of compliment to his associates, Mr. Rogers called the Buffalo and Susquehanna Iron Company."[6]

It was only natural, given the extensive interlocking relationships that existed among Buffalo's dominant industrialists, that all of these "fellow travelers"— Rogers, the Goodyear brothers, Edmund Hayes, and John J. Albright—became members of the founding board of directors of the Marine National.

The Marine National Bank was a critical part of the infrastructure of the modern industrial system that was transforming Buffalo. It was a way to guarantee that money flowed "from where it was to where it was most needed and would do the most good," an anonymous member of the board of the new bank told the *Buffalo Commercial*.[7] (Could that have been John J. Albright?) Albany, he said, "has long since ceased to be a town where industries flourish. It is dead except while the legislature is in session. And yet," he continued, "there is a vast amount of wealth there. The banks are choked with it … there is much more money in Albany than can be used there." Pointing to the Marine National, our interviewee said, "In Buffalo we can't get the money that we need." But "if a big bank were organized in Buffalo and close relationships between it and

Faces of Power in turn-of-the-century Buffalo. Clockwise from top left: William H. Gratwick, Edmund B. Hayes, Charles W. Goodyear, Frank H. Goodyear.

Courtesy of The Buffalo History Museum, used by permission

Albany were established, it would be possible to use Albany's surplus wealth for the purpose of financing and building up great industries here."[8]

An immediate and powerful connection was established between the new bank and the new steel company, Lackawanna Iron and Steel. Indeed, the timing of these two most important events suggests that they might well have been planned and implemented simultaneously. The press was frank in its reporting. *The Buffalo Express* noted:

> *The close relations existing between the Marine National Bank and the Lackawanna Steel Company and some of the foremost financiers in the country were shown yesterday when the bank announced the increase in its board of directors from eight to fifteen and the increase of its capital and surplus to $1,500,000, with undivided profits of $250,000.*[9]

Added to the existing board of Albright, Hayes, and Frank Goodyear were Goodyear's brother Charles, Walter Scranton, national steel magnate Moses Taylor, and, perhaps the biggest "fish" of all, Cornelius Vanderbilt of New York City. Each was a member of Lackawanna's board of directors. *The Express* unapologetically wrote about the participation of these "outside capitalists": "D. O. Mills is a multimillionaire, one of the richest men in America. Mr. Iselin is of the old and established house of Iselin and Company. The Taylors are millionaires many times over." Without any sense that the move towards outside ownership of the local industrial infrastructure might at some point prove portentous, the *Express* continued confidently:

"It means much to Buffalo to have these men of many millions and vast interest and influence become directly involved in the financial life of this city."[10]

The creation of the Marine National Bank quickly realized its mission. In the first year after receiving its charter and entering the national banking system in 1902, deposits increased by $5,000,000. J. N. Larned, the great turn-of-the century chronicler of Buffalo's history, touted the bank's success: "In 1906 its accumulated surplus, exceeding $2,000,000, was partly capitalized by an enlargement of capital stock from $230,000 to $1,500,000 … A recent financial statement of the bank to the Comptroller of the Currency showed $17,056,495 deposits with a surplus and profits of $1,182,883."[11] Clearly, John J. Albright and his colleagues and partners had reason to be proud of and pleased with their accomplishment.

Albright's involvement with these two banks reflects his sophisticated understanding not only of the workings of the new industrial economy but of the rapidly changing urban environment. Despite his fascination with architectural historicism, he was a forerunner of modernism in his disregard for actual history. In his desire to build a thoroughly modern city, he had no use for and saw no value in preserving Buffalo's existing, but rapidly vanishing, streetscape. While not a preservation movement as such, a growing number of people in Buffalo had become increasingly concerned about the encroachment of railroads on the traditional streetscape and the creep of commerce on what Frank Severance, secretary of the Buffalo Historical Society and the era's leading "preservationist" called a "vanished Main Street."[12] Though Andrew Langdon, the brother of Albright's late wife, Harriet, was president of the Historical Society and therefore undoubtedly knew Severance, Albright held no such sentimental beliefs about preserving and protecting Buffalo's radically changing urban landscape. In fact, it was Albright and the other officers and directors of the Equitable Trust who, over the objections of many, ordered that the much-loved Weed Block be demolished: the lot that it had occupied since mid-century was needed for their new bank building.

The Weed Block, designed by a well-known mid-century architect named Calvin N. Otis, had stood at the southwest corner of Main and Swan Streets since 1857. Here, former US Presidents Millard Fillmore and Grover Cleveland had once located their offices. From the Weed Block, a reporter for the *Buffalo Courier* wrote in 1901, "Many letters and messages were sent which have had the greatest bearing on the life of the nation." In February 1901, Fidelity Trust bought the block and announced their plans to demolish it. E. B. Green, Buffalo's brilliant and increasingly omnipresent architect, had been retained to design their new headquarters. In November 1901, Green filed his plans: "At a cost of $750,000, the new structure will be ten stories high and will be one of the finest buildings in the city."[13]

Notwithstanding a sense of disappointment about its pending demolition, the culture of the times celebrated the promise of the future. While recognizing the historical interest and value of the Weed Block, the article contended, "The chances are that in the building that the Fidelity Trust will erect, history will continue to be made."[14]

Four years after Fidelity's new building opened in 1909, Green was commissioned to design another modern office building just down Main Street from the Equitable, this one a sixteen-story tower for Albright's Marine National Bank. Driven by their desire to rationalize the world in which they worked, Albright and his colleagues created not only modern banking structures but modern buildings in which to house them.

Above and beyond a national bank, what the industrial capitalists of America wanted and needed even more was a central bank with an elastic currency, one that would provide stability and emergency credit in times of financial crisis. For that, they would not have to wait long. In the wake of the Panic of 1907, increasing demands were heard for the creation of such a bank—a "Federal Reserve Bank," it was being called.

As momentum gathered, Rhode Island Senator Nelson Aldrich, a leading advocate for such a bank, in 1910 convened a secret meeting of New York City's leading bankers at a millionaires' hideaway on Jekyll Island. Founded in the late 1880s, Jekyll boasted an elite and exclusive roster of members including Marshall Field, John Pierpont Morgan, Joseph Pulitzer, and William K. Vanderbilt, each of whom had homes there. And it was to Jekyll Island in the middle of the night of November 22, 1910, on a private train that left Hoboken, New Jersey, shrouded in secrecy, that Senator Aldrich and a handful of men went: A. P. Andrews, Assistant Secretary of the United States Treasury Department; Paul Warburg of Kuhn, Loeb Investment company; Frank A. Vanderlip, president of the National City Bank of New York; Henry P. Davison, senior partner of J. P. Morgan Company;

Charles D. Norton, president of the Morgan-dominated First National Bank of New York; and Benjamin Strong, representing Morgan. Together, these passengers on Aldrich's train represented about one fourth of the world's wealth at the time. And this clandestine journey led to the drafting of what three years later would become the Federal Reserve Act.[15]

Although he was not along on that fateful ride, is it too farfetched to assume that, when they arrived at Jekyll two days later, the guests might have been greeted there by John J. Albright, who for years, along with Buffalonians Edmund B. Hayes and the Goodyear brothers, had been wintering in a large apartment at the Jekyll Island Club? We don't know with certainty if John Albright was at these meetings, but given the life that he had led, the businesses that he had founded, and, in particular, the banking crises that he had faced, plus the fact that he was a member of the club, it makes sense to believe that this time, anyway, he was there.

SIX

Electrical Power

The first power plant built at Niagara Falls in August 1895 was owned and developed not by John J. Albright, but rather by Jacob Schoellkopf. In the florid but accurate words of Josephus Larned, "The transformation into electrical energy of some part of the stupendous force of gravitation which is spent in the fall of the mighty Niagara," was an event of extraordinary and unprecedented significance in Buffalo's history.[1] And Albright knew it. In April 1900, three months after announcing his gift to the Buffalo Society of Artists, Albright acquired the Ontario Power Company, a struggling Canadian business, and transformed it into the largest endeavor of its kind on the Canadian side of the Niagara River. Along with this purchase came the right to draw up to 360,000 horsepower from the river, guaranteed by the Canadian government.[2]

Albright's grandson Birge reports that his grandfather was able to secure an agreement with the Queen Victoria Park Commissioners who, in exchange for $15,000 a year in rent, granted Albright's Ontario Power Company the rights to develop 400,000 horsepower of water from the Niagara River. Albright's operation, wrote Birge, was extraordinary and unique. For unlike Schoellkopf's Niagara Falls Hydraulic, the Ontario Power Company drew its water from the Niagara River above the falls. From there it was conveyed over a mile in large pipes through Queen Victoria Park, plunging down the 235-foot drop at the falls to the power plant at the base. It was a vast project involving the utmost planning, requiring Albright to draw on all of the engineering expertise that his education and background had provided him.

Certainly, the effort to create the new power company was herculean and the amount of effort, energy, and thought that was involved in its creation was staggering. Think of it: a new company, in new country, using a new system for the generation of power that required a new and different kind of industrial infrastructure. What were the working dynamics of this fascinating new venture? How did Albright put this most complex deal together? How was it financed? What was the nature of these financial arrangements? How were the licensing agreements between the provincial government of Ontario and the OPC made? Did John J. Albright do all of this work? Did he supervise it? If so, how? Was he in the field, trudging up and down the steep ravines amidst the rapidly coursing waters of the Niagara River as they crashed over the Horseshoe Falls? What do we know about the relationships between these most intriguing men: John Albright, George Westinghouse, and Nikola Tesla? What were the roles of the officers and directors, men whose names are inseparable from Albright's? People like Francis V. Greene; William E. Gratwick; the

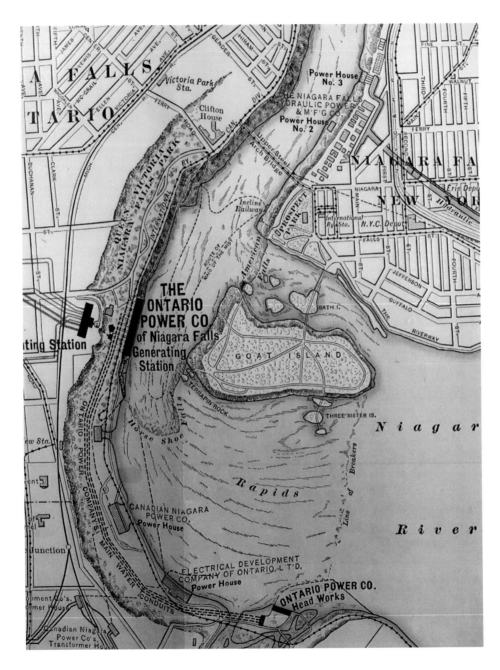

The location of the Ontario Power Company at Niagara Falls, Ontario.

Niagara Falls Ontario Public Library, used with permission

4766 - DISTRIBUTING STATION - JULY 15, 1912

Ontario Power Company Distributing Station, designed by
E.B. Green, completed in 1906.

Niagara Falls Ontario Public Library, used with permission

Goodyear brothers; Stephen M. Clement, a cofounder with Albright of the Marine National Bank; and the omnipresent Edmund Hayes who, like E. B. Green, was seemingly always at Albright's side.[3] How helpful and instructive it would be, what wonderful insight we would have into the gritty, yet staggeringly complex mechanics that were at the foundation of the modern American economy, had the great man himself left even the slightest shred of information or recorded his thoughts on these critical topics.

He did seem, however, to waste little time. Within four years Ontario Power had built a powerhouse below the Horseshoe Falls and laid the first of three 1.8 kilometer-long intake conduits. By 1905, the first units of the plant had entered service. Housed in a complex of E. B. Green-designed buildings (imagine the skills and breadth of vision of this architect who simultaneously was designing both a Greek Revival art gallery and an electrical power complex), the building of the OPC was an extraordinary achievement. Paul Nunn, one of the nation's leading electrical engineers, whom Albright hired to work alongside Green, described its layout in detail, with a particular fascination with numbers:

From the head-gates of the Ontario Company, three great steel-and-concrete tunnels or conduits beneath the surface of the park will convey nearly 12,000 cubic feet of water per sec. to the top of the cliff above the powerhouse. Thence it will pass through 22 steel penstocks in shafts and tunnels down and out through the cliff to an equal number of horizontal turbines in the powerhouse below. From the

generators the electrical cables turn back through tunnels to the 22 banks of switches, transformers, and instruments of the distributing station above and to the transmission lines beyond, completing equipment for more than 200,000 horsepower.[4]

The complex of buildings overlooking the Canadian falls that John J. Albright created and that E. B. Green designed was the largest grouping of industrial buildings since the construction of Lackawanna Steel several years earlier. It included a gatehouse, a switching station, several substations, and a generating plant which, one commentator noted, was "a dignified structure of unobtrusive design, that so harmonized in color with the cliff at its back that it cannot always be distinguished through the spray from the cliff itself."[5]

Ontario Power was also praised for its methods of operation, particularly Albright's willingness and ability to delegate critical engineering questions and concerns to the experts he hired for the company. In a paper delivered in 1905, Paul Nunn made the following remark:

More than all else in the establishment of this great and daring enterprise stands out the attitude maintained toward their engineers by Messrs. J. J. Albright and Edmund Hayes who, in strong contrast with the harassing interference by which uninformed investors frequently spoil the best efforts of engineers, have in this case given not only absolute freedom of action, but also steadfast support.[6]

The impact, as the *Buffalo Express* noted when OPC opened in January 1905, was immediate and momentous: "The harnessing of Niagara caused a wonder but the transmission of Niagara power—the placing of Niagara power on a wire and delivering it to every considerable market within a 250-mile radius is the second wonder, one greater than the first, for Niagara has entered on the transmission era."[7]

In a direct reference to the work that Albright had overseen, the newspaper noted, "The transmission age at Niagara involves some of the greatest feats of engineering, some of the most considerable outlays of capital, some of the most far-reaching industrial changes, the center of which is Buffalo, that have ever been or will be seen."[8]

Armed with the capability to produce electrical power, Albright now sought the capacity to transmit it. At this time one of the world's largest transmission companies was the Niagara, Lockport, Ontario Power Company, founded by George Westinghouse in 1894. At the time of its founding, Westinghouse entered into a licensing agreement with New York State that allowed the company to draw an unlimited amount of water from the Niagara River for the purposes of transmitting electrical power. Westinghouse's plan was to divert water from the Niagara River, channel it via a fourteen-mile-long canal to a power plant in Lockport from where, following its use, the water would flow via 18 Mile Creek into Lake Ontario. Westinghouse's agreement with the state gave his company ten years to begin work on the project.

Westinghouse's finances were shaky and work was progressing slowly when, just before the license was to run out in 1904, a group of investors led by John J. Albright purchased control of the company. The details of that purchase, revealed in a 1906 document housed in the local history collection of the Niagara Falls, Ontario, public library, are fascinating. In an extraordinary transaction, OPC sold bonds valued at $3 million (more than $75 million today) to the Toronto General Trust Company. The terms were generous: the bonds were not due until 1921, annual installments were low, and no personal guarantees were required. These terms gave Albright and his team the time and the cash needed to develop their company. And they did. In 1906, Albright acquired outright the Niagara, Lockport and Ontario Power Company which now had the exclusive right to distribute the 180,000 horsepower of electricity produced by OPC as far away as Syracuse. That distance—more than 180 miles—was among the longest in the world.

Electrical transmissions began in early 1905. The reactions in the press were ecstatic. From the *Buffalo Express*: "The first inkling of the change to the transmission era at Niagara is seen in the transmissions of the Niagara, Lockport and Ontario Power Company. Few people have realized the gigantic nature of this transmission, which is by far the greatest in the world. This company, which may be considered almost a Buffalo concern, derives its power from the Ontario Power Company, which has rights for more horsepower than any company in the world."[9] The absence of Albright's name in this article is noteworthy.

An undated publication in the Niagara Falls, Ontario, public library outlines "what that power was used for." The list is long and includes, but is not limited to, part or all of the public and private lighting in Niagara Falls, Welland, and St. Catherine's in Ontario, and Lockport, Depew, West Seneca, Hamburg, Batavia, Rochester, Canandaigua, Auburn, Fulton, and Syracuse in New York State; trolley systems in Syracuse, Rochester, Canandaigua, West Seneca, and Hamburg, as well as interurban lines between Buffalo and Syracuse. The article continues: "It operates the steel works of the Ontario Iron and Steel Company in Welland, the Lackawanna Steel Company, the Shenandoah Steel Company, the repair shops of the New York Central Railroad, and various smaller industries located along main transmission lines." The report concludes: "Through the distributing systems of light, heat, and power companies in various cities throughout Ontario and New York, this power is applied to practically every use for which power is utilized, from sewing machines and ventilating fans to rolling mills and trip hammers."[10]

What was so carefully constructed was remarkably easily threatened. Suddenly, "with no warning," as Albright's attorney Franklin D. Locke described it, all of Albright's efforts to generate and transmit power from the Niagara River to Buffalo, Rochester, Syracuse, and beyond were frighteningly jeopardized. In January 1906, Ohio Congressman Theodore Burton, chairman of the House Committee on Rivers and Harbors, at the behest of President Theodore Roosevelt, convened his committee to consider legislation that would curb considerably the amount of water that power companies could divert from the Niagara River.

For years there had been growing concerns about the impact of development on the future of the falls as an international scenic destination. Beginning in the mid-1880s, New York State had granted charters to seven different companies to divert water from the Niagara River just above the falls. Commercial activity continued so that by 1904 five different companies, according to one historian, were

> … *blasting through Niagara limestone to create a labyrinth of underground diversion tunnels and deep trenches to house giant turbines … Above ground, cranes and shovels cut into the gorge at the foot of the Falls and excavated sites along the upper rapids above the Falls for massive powerhouse structures and the land encompassing the Falls underwent a breathtaking transformation that stunned the world.*[11]

Conservationists, citing the absence of any limits on the amount of water that the NLOPC was allowed to transmit, now accused the state of "handing out free diversion permits." The attacks on the power companies were harsh. If the falls were to be saved "from our over-eager commercialism," it was necessary, many argued, to drastically limit the amount of water that could be legally diverted. J. Horace McFarland, president of the American Civic Association, a leading national organization for the improvement and beautification of America's cities, was among the most ardent proponents of limiting, if not ending, the diversion of Niagara River water for the purpose of creating electrical power. "Niagara Falls," he said, "belongs to the world" and "the sordid materialism of an insignificant minority who are willing to sacrifice Niagara Falls for the purposes of dividends … should not be allowed to prevail." McFarland continued: "I speak for the millions who have evidenced their feelings in this matter most

Power lines belonging to Albright's Ontario Power Corporation, circa 1907. These lines and the associated towers infuriated those who felt they despoiled Niagara Falls.

Niagara Falls Ontario Public Library, used with permission

strongly that the Falls must not be allowed to be overrun with every species of abominable fungus. All that we believe in is comprised in two words: Save Niagara." [12]

McFarland was harsh in his criticism of E. B. Green's powerhouse for the Ontario Power Company: "You have had prepared for you an adornment for Niagara in the form of a great powerhouse built in the Italian Renaissance style. Ye Gods, Niagara has waited all these years to have an Italian Renaissance adornment added to her majesty?" [13] Others felt differently. Josephus Larned, the noted Buffalo historian writing in 1910, declared that Green's buildings, unlike the others, were designed and constructed so that "the whole conveyance of water to it is out of sight, underground, and the other structures connected with the plant are not only of pleasing architecture, but too far removed to affect the scenic framing of the Falls." [14]

In his most biting critique of the impact of the unlimited diversion of water on Niagara Falls, McFarland cited a cartoon from *Puck Magazine* in which "Niagara Falls is shown as a great precipice, the falls being dry. The Cave of the Winds is shown as a cave under where the falls once poured their waters and where ice-cream is now sold. There is also a little place where you can buy genuine Niagara water for 5 cents a glass. The Maid of the Mist is an automobile and runs along the dry river bed and shows you the scenery." Predicting the end of Niagara Falls as a global destination, McFarland said: "For who will come to see a bare cliff and a mass of factories, a maze of tunnels, wires, wheels and generators?" [15]

Albright was deeply concerned about the tone and direction of the Burton hearings, and at sessions held in Washington, DC, in early 1906, his lawyers, Franklin Locke, formerly John Milburn's partner in Milburn and Locke; and Paul Cravath, "the J. P. Morgan of the New York City bar," fought back. (Was Albright in attendance, sitting quietly, as was his wont?)

Locke went first. "Just now," he said, "there is a public sentiment upon this side [referring to the American side, as the Canadians at that time were far less eager to impede the commercial development of the falls] to preserve the Falls even at the expense of ruining the power companies." Locke protested that the effect of the proposed Burton Bill would be "to drive industries, the manufactured products of which would amount to hundreds of thousands of millions a year, from the US to Canada … We do not wish to destroy the sentimental or the beautiful about Niagara Falls but we do wish to preserve our property and property rights."

Locke was adamant, arguing that the company had done all that the law required of it: "We have applied to the War Department to find out how we should get across the Niagara River, and the War Department advised us that they had no jurisdiction over it. So we strung our wires across the Niagara." In addition, Locke argued that his client had "applied to the Treasury Department, and we were advised by them that electricity is not subject to customs law and that there was no limit on the amount that can be imported. So we went ahead with our construction, built our canal and our lines, and we made a contract with the Ontario Power Corporation to buy and transmit their power." Locke was angry:

Puck Cartoon, 1906. This picture is worth a thousand words.

Courtesy of Douglas Levere, Buffalo, NY

Now comes this bolt out of the blue. Stop right here you say. Although you have made your contracts, although you have made your construction for that purpose. We have gone in good faith and have built our works. We have put out our securities; we have sold our bonds; we have spent millions of dollars to carry out our contracts … I maintain that you are trying to shut us off.

Next to testify on behalf of Albright's power interests was the renowned corporate defense attorney Paul P. Cravath, who demurred to the growing regulatory sentiment. "The assumption is sound," he said, "that there is a strong demand on the part of the people for adequate means to preserve the scenic beauty of Niagara Falls and that in some way and in some form that wish will be finally given expression." Cravath then proceeded to document the extent of the work that Albright's two companies had already undertaken. He cited Lackawanna Steel, "whose enormous plant at South Buffalo depends exclusively on my client's current for its power. We have, in addition, the New York Central Railroad that has agreed to use our power exclusively for its electrical lines." He continued, emphasizing the length, breadth, and reach of the commitments that Albright and his partners had made:

The industries which have made arrangements to utilize our current involve hundreds of millions of dollars. Indeed, it may be said that the whole industrial activities of that part of New York State center around the utilization of the current of this company. We have entered into firm contracts for the sale of this power, and we have also in every

important case subjected ourselves to heavy penalties in case we fail to deliver the power within reasonable time.

Cravath maintained that his client was shocked and appalled:

We believe that the amount of water to be diverted would not materially affect the scenic beauty of Niagara Falls. We knew that the river was not navigable at that point where we are taking the water. We knew that no question of interstate commerce or navigation was involved and that therefore there was no federal jurisdiction. We believed that we had made every honest and sincere effort to create this business, having spent in excess of $4 million.

Cravath, summing up the position of his client, implored: "The enactment of such a bill as you propose, if it could be enforced, would ruin my client; it would destroy his investment because this investment is of absolutely no value except for the purposes of utilizing the power which we in time expect to generate." [16]

Albright's lawyers were not the only ones who questioned the wisdom of the Burton Bill. An editorial in *Popular Mechanics*, a very popular journal at the time, questioned the basic assumptions of the bill and its priorities that put scenic beauty above the enormous savings created by producing power from water as opposed to coal. Arguing that the amount of coal needed annually to equal the 3.5 million horsepower available at Niagara Falls would cost the country $122 million per year, *Popular Mechanics* pointed out, "These figures illustrate what it actually costs the people of this continent to maintain Niagara Falls as a spectacle." The editorial concluded, seemingly puzzled, "From the number of petitions and the general agitation of the subject, it seems that the American people are still willing to pay that price."[17]

But such arguments were not enough, and in June 1906 the Burton Bill became law. It removed the permit-granting power from the New York State legislature, putting it instead in the hands of the Secretary of War. In addition, it limited to three years the total flow of water available for diversion and called for a treaty with Canada to settle the matter permanently. Over the next several years as negotiations dragged on, public interest flagged and the pressure of the power companies increased. While conservationists hoped that a treaty would limit diversions to the existing actual usage of 34,000 cubic feet per second, the power companies asked for and received permission to divert 56,000 cubic feet, a limit that was maintained until 1950.[18]

Despite his concerns about the impact of the Burton Bill, Albright survived the outcome. Following its passage, he built a steam plant at Lyons, New York, at which the power of the Salmon River in Upstate New York, not far from his home at Wilmurt, was harnessed. Power from the Oswego River was obtained and a transmission line, "at that time the largest one in the world," was completed. By 1910, Albright's companies had approximately 400 miles of transmission lines running from Niagara Falls through Lockport and Rochester to Syracuse, a total distance of 167 miles from the distributing station. In 1913, he completed his buy-out of the Westinghouse interests, becoming the largest stockholder of the Niagara, Lockport and Ontario Power Company. He celebrated his prosperity one year later by buying the largest home on Jekyll Island, the twenty-six-room "cottage" that had been owned by publisher-philanthropist Joseph Pulitzer. Then, in 1915, he sold the Ontario Power Company to the Province of Ontario for $5,000,000, more than $125,000,000 in 2017 dollars.

Other than Birge Albright's enlightening discussion of Albright's work on the creation and generation of electrical power, I have yet to unearth any primary source material that either documents or attests to the towering role that Albright himself played in these developments. While there are hints and suggestions here and there, like the rare and slight reference above to the "Vanderbilt, Westinghouse, Albright, and Hayes" connection, there is nothing substantial, no correspondence between and among the principals, no bills of lading, nothing other than Birge's account that puts John Albright, clearly and unquestionably, at the scene. Here, as in all other aspects of his life, he remains largely an enigma. In business and in philanthropy and even in the work for which he is best known in Buffalo, the creation of the Albright Art Gallery, we need to dig deep to prove that he was really there.

SEVEN

The Albright Art Gallery

In 1887, five years after his move to Buffalo, Albright began the first of what would become many terms as a member of the board of directors of the Buffalo Fine Arts Academy. He served as vice-president in 1894 and as president between 1895 and 1897. According to an early history of the Buffalo Fine Arts Academy written in 1899, Albright, in addition to establishing a scholarship for the Art Students League of Buffalo, organized "one of the most interesting exhibitions ever held in Buffalo."[1] The exhibition consisted, according to Birge Albright, of the paintings that Albright favored, the mid-nineteenth-century French landscape artists known as the Barbizon school, whose dark, quiet, and romantic depictions of everyday country life appealed greatly to him.

Although founded in1862, the Buffalo Fine Arts Academy did not have a home of its own. Rather, like the Buffalo Academy of Natural Sciences and the Buffalo Historical Society, it shared space with other "culturals" in the Central Library on Lafayette Square in downtown Buffalo. Given Albright's lofty ambitions and his eagerness to commission new and striking buildings, it is no wonder that he would not be satisfied with the modest, even—as the sign that hung on the exterior of the library in an 1890 photograph suggests—shabby quarters that it shared with others at the Central Library.

It is likely that, in the mid-1890s as his clearly growing resources allowed, Albright began to conceive of what would become by 1905 the Albright Art Gallery.

Suddenly, without fanfare or prior indication, in 1900 John J. Albright announced that he would build a brand new home for the Buffalo Fine Arts Academy. In what would become the most public statement of his long career, Albright outlined his plans. In a letter to the president of the academy board, his long-term business partner and fellow RPI alumnus, T. Guilford Smith, and published by the *Buffalo Express*, Albright offered the details of his extraordinary gift:

As a lover of art and a believer in its beneficent influence in such a city as ours, I have long felt that the academy could not fulfill the purposes of its founders and friends without the possession of a permanent and suitable home. Such a home should be exclusively devoted to art, and its architecture and surroundings should of itself represent the nature of its occupancy. From such inquiries as I have been able to make, I am led to believe that a suitable building would cost from $300,000 to $350,000. This expenditure I am ready to meet.[2]

By the time the gallery was completed in 1905, Albright had contributed closer to $1 million, about $26 million in 2016 dollars.

The Buffalo Public Library, circa 1890. It was in this extraordinary building that the Buffalo Fine Arts Academy was housed prior to the construction of Mr. Albright's Gallery. Note the sign "Water Color Exhibition. Admission 25 cents" over the main door.

From Buffalo 1890. *The Mark Goldman collection*

New Buildings in Buffalo—Albright Art Gallery to Cost $1,000,000, Gift of a Buffalo Citizen—As It Looks Today.

—Photo by Oscar A. Simon.

ALBRIGHT ART GALLERY, DELAWARE PARK, BUFFALO, N.Y.   8979

TOP: A newspaper image of The Albright Gallery, three years before it opened. Photograph by Oscar A. Simon.
Reproduction by permission of the Grosvenor Room, Buffalo & Erie County Public Library, Buffalo, NY

BOTTOM: Colorized postcard of the Albright Art Gallery.
Reproduction by permission of the Grosvenor Room, Buffalo & Erie County Public Library, Buffalo, NY

Other than insisting that the building "should be of white marble," he said nothing about architectural style. What concerned him more was that the building, like those depicted in the Barbizon landscapes that he so admired, be located in a pristine environment, "remote from other buildings for all time." Consistent with the ideals of the turn-of-the century City Beautiful school of city planning, Albright wanted to be sure that the new gallery was "removed from all risk of injury because of the proximity of manufacturing plants, apartment houses, or any other use of adjacent property as might tend to impair the effect of the structure." For this reason he insisted that the building be located in Delaware Park: "I do not know how this condition can be met in our growing city unless the site be within the public park." Concerned about the sustainability of his gallery, Albright advised (whether this was a suggestion or a requirement is not clear) that the maintenance fund of the academy be increased from its then current $28,000 (this was not an annual amount, but rather the amount of cash on hand) "to such an amount that the institution will have a clear ample income for the maintenance of its structure."[3]

While Albright's letter reveals that he believed in the "beneficent influence of art in a city such as ours," there is nothing in the record, nothing even in the archives of his eponymous gallery that would help us to learn more about and to better understand his momentous decision. What was he thinking in January 1900 when he offered his staggering gift? In what ways did he understand art to have a "beneficent influence" on the life of the city? What role did his new wife, Susan, play? Was the idea of a museum for Buffalo something that Albright discussed with his business colleagues—people like Edmund Hayes and Frank Goodyear, partners in business, who also served alongside Albright as members of the board throughout most of the new gallery's first years?

To what extent was he influenced by his young architect, E. B. Green? Again, in the absence of any correspondence between these two men who did so much to shape the landscape of the city that we live in today, we are led to conjecture. What kinds of instructions did Albright give his architect? Did he tell him to build in the Greek Revival style that the building came to embody? In an undated account carefully stored in the archives is a fragment of a document in which "Mr. Green told of the many trips that he made under Mr. Albright's direction to inspect various art buildings throughout the county to gather the best ideas from the foremost architects."[4]

But where did he go? What buildings did he visit? Though not completed until 1904, there is a chance that Green had seen McKim, Mead and White's sketches for the new Greek Revival façade and entranceway that they were working on for the Metropolitan Museum of Art. Although that firm's Museum of Fine Arts in Boston was available for Green's inspection, its Renaissance façade seems to have had little if any impact on him. To a certain extent Albright and Green were working in a vacuum. In the US at least, the construction of large, stand-alone art museums that we have come to associate with major cities was, if not in its infancy, certainly in its early days. Although New York had its Metropolitan and Boston its Museum of Fine Arts, Philadelphia did not have a dedicated building for its museum of fine arts until the 1920s.

It was a closer look at Raymond K. Albright's photographs that led me to the true source of his father's inspiration for the Albright Art Gallery. Among the hundreds of Raymond's photographs, carefully arranged in two long boxes housed in the collections department of the George Eastman Museum, are several that he took of the Acropolis, each looking remarkably like the art gallery that John J. Albright would build in Buffalo nearly a decade later.

When the Albright Gallery was finally completed in 1905 (after a long delay related to difficulties in the acquisition and transportation of the more than 100 marble columns required by Green's design), the building was, according to a leading critic of the time, "the finest example of pure Greek architecture to be found in America." [5]

The opening ceremonies—photographed and at times later displayed in large format in the gallery's café—were held on May 31, 1905, at what was then the gallery's main entrance overlooking the lake in Delaware Park. The ceremony began at four o'clock in the afternoon when, according to *Academy Notes*, a gallery publication, "The Directors of the Buffalo Fine Arts Academy and those who were to participate in the ceremonies marched from the park casino to reserved seats near the speakers' stand, and the exercises began. Mr. Ralph H. Plumb, president of the Academy presided. First came the singing by the Orpheus, Sangerbund, Teutonia Liederkrantz and the Guido Society [the choruses that represented Italian, German, and Polish immigrant communities] of Beethoven's impressive chorus, "The Heavens are telling of the Lord's endless glory." Then President Charles William Eliot of Harvard University was introduced and

A fascinating photograph taken by Raymond Albright during the family's Grand Tour. It is not of the Acropolis but rather of a Neo-Classical knock-off of the Acropolis: the Academy of Athens built in 1885. John J. Albright must certainly have shared this photograph with his architect, E.B. Green when, ten years after his return from Europe, Albright began to think about building the gallery. (Information on the Academy courtesy of Colin Dabkowski)

Courtesy of George Eastman Museum

An extraordinary photograph of the May 31, 1905 dedication of the brand new Albright Art Gallery. Founder and benefactor John J. Albright is hidden, sitting just out of sight in the photo on the top right. Found in one of Susan Fuller Albright's albums, it is safe to say that Susan herself took this photo. The mechanics as well as the psychodynamics of this are fascinating to consider.

delivered an address on "Beauty and Democracy" … Mr. Richard Watson Gilder, being next introduced, read the dedicatory poem entitled "A Temple of Art." Later the gallery was thrown upon to the public and several thousand persons enjoyed the inaugural loan exhibition, which was a remarkable collection of more than two hundred old and modern paintings."[6]

John Albright was barely visible at the ceremony. He neither spoke nor sat with those who did, sitting largely unobserved, as ever enigmatic, in the third row in the middle of the crowd. *The Buffalo Evening News* reported, "He would not accept a seat more distinguished than those shared by his fellow directors."[7] Not a note, not a photograph, not a fragment from him, let alone an interview with the man himself, has been found that suggests what John Albright was thinking on this magnificent afternoon in May 1905.

August St. Gaudens, the great American sculptor who Albright had commissioned to design the eight caryatids that would soon grace the building's exterior, was at the event and thought the new gallery was spectacular, particularly at night: "Have you ever seen the Albright Art Gallery by moonlight? It is one of the most beautiful sights I have ever seen." Of the gallery itself he said that "it is the best lighted gallery in the world, one of the finest buildings of its kind in the entire country."[8] A writer for *Academy Notes* was more poetic still: "The white marble art palace, rising out of the mass of variegated greens into an Italian blue sky, seemed to express a purer beauty and more impressive dignity than ever before."[9]

Cornelia Bentley Sage, assistant to the Albright's first director, Charles M. Kurtz, a woman whose relationship with the Albright family would become long and intimate, captured the essence of what twenty-five years later would be referred to as Albright's "unpretentious social conduct" and "simple greatness." In a poem that she wrote at the gallery opening titled "Gloria Mundi," Miss Sage included an unveiled reference to Albright:

> *Of him whose generous impulse gave thee birth?*
> *What shall we say of him? Our temple's fame*
> *Outrivals the fame of Greece! But he who builds for*
> *other men hath greater worth*
> *Than kings and councilors—a nobler name*
> *Than princes, for he builds unselfishly.*[10]

The inaugural exhibition of June 1905 included 237 paintings and pieces of sculpture, 231 of them on loan from museums and galleries all over the country. According to Birge Albright, Albright himself was involved in curating the inaugural show, traveling to New York and Montreal with Kurtz and Ralph Plumb, president of the Fine Arts Academy, to select works. In New York, Birge reports, the trio was able to persuade the Metropolitan Museum to lend Manet's *Boy with Sword* in addition to works by Velasquez, Delacroix, and other old world masters.

The gallery's first traveling exhibition, held in January 1906, was entitled "Selected Paintings of American Artists," featuring the work of James McNeill Whistler, William Merritt Chase, George Inness, and others. Later that year, Kurtz arranged for the first exhibition in America of contemporary German paintings. Two years later, the gallery staged an exhibition of French impressionist painters including Pissarro,

Monet, Renoir, and Degas. An article in the *Buffalo Express* referred to the exhibition as the "finest small collection of the works of the impressionists shown in America up to the present time."[11] We wonder: did Albright, perhaps a budding modernist, help to curate this show?

We do know that Albright's taste in art was traditional and conservative. He was particularly drawn to the small group of American painters who made their home in New Hampshire at a place known as The Dublin Colony. One of them was George de Forest Brush who Albright met at the Pan-American Exposition. In 1902 Albright commissioned Brush to paint a portrait of Susan Fuller Albright and her three oldest children. Filled with classical references, this portrait, a highly romantic hymn to motherhood, became part of the Albright's permanent collection in 1934 when George Cary bought it and gave it to the gallery.

Charles Kurtz was particularly interested in photography, and sometime in the early years of the century, after he'd been appointed director of the Albright Art Gallery, he initiated a correspondence with Alfred Stieglitz, the great American photographer and founder of the Photo-Secession school of photography. In late winter of 1909, Kurtz travelled to New York (did he take with him his assistant, Miss Sage? Or John Albright's wife, Susan Fuller Albright, or Charlotte Spaulding Albright, Albright's new daughter-in-law, both of whom were avid photographers)? He met with Stieglitz at his gallery at 291 Fifth Avenue to plan what would become the first museum show ever of the avant-garde photographic work known as Photo-Pictorialism. We can guess that when Kurtz's attention

turned to photography, it is likely that he had the support of Albright's wife.

Photography was in the air in turn-of-the-century Buffalo. The Buffalo Camera Club, formed in 1888 with the goal of advancing among its members "the knowledge of photography in all its branches," had by 1900 approximately forty members.[12] Although the club made no distinction between amateur and professional photographers, they were clear in their distinction between men and women: the latter were not admitted to membership. Nevertheless, photography, particularly portrait photography, had by the late 1890s become an avocation, and in some cases a vocation, for a small group of highly talented female photographers including Rose Clark, Clara Sipprell, and, of particular importance to our story, Charlotte Spaulding. By the turn of the century these women had come under the influence of Alfred Stieglitz, who, working out of New York City, gave rise not only to what he called the Photo-Secession but also to a spin-off of that known as "photo pictorialism." Stieglitz's energetic trumpeting of photography as an art form struck a powerful chord within Buffalo's photographic community. Between 1902 and 1904, the Buffalo Camera Club sponsored two exhibitions at their offices in the Market Arcade building on Main Street, devoted to a "collection of artistic pictures"[13]

Committed to "creating" an image rather than simply recording it, the photo pictorialists made soft, largely out-of-focus images in hopes of projecting emotions rather than reality. Female photographers were, it seemed, particularly drawn to this new and emerging art form. By the mid-1890s, several working in Buffalo were making haunting, shadowy, and mysterious photographs, mostly portraits. One of these women was Charlotte Spaulding, who in 1908 was to become, as the wife of Langdon Albright, John Albright's daughter-in-law. Another was Albright's second wife, Susan Fuller who, in 1900, began an intensive photographic study of her family that lasted for at least a quarter of a century.

These Albright in-laws were not, as our earlier discussion of son Raymond's circa 1888 travel photographs prove, the first members of the family to demonstrate an interest in photography. It is highly likely then that, given what was clearly a strong family interest in photography, the Albrights were enthusiastic supporters of the efforts of first Charles Kurtz and then Cornelia Bentley Sage to bring Stieglitz's Photo-Secession show to the gallery.

Susan Fuller Albright's interest in photography and her husband's role at the newly opened Albright Art Gallery must certainly have put her in contact with Cornelia Bentley Sage. Following the sudden death of Charles Kurtz in March 1909, Miss Sage assumed the job of acting director and in 1910 was appointed director, the first such position ever held by a woman in the US. She is an important and fascinating character in the history of the twentieth-century art museum. During her years as director, between 1910 and 1924, she played a significant role in shaping the development of the gallery. Born in Buffalo in 1876 (she was eight years younger than Susan Fuller), she graduated from the Buffalo Seminary, a highly regarded female academy, and continued her studies at the Art Students League of Buffalo, forerunner of the Albright

A Catalog of the 1910 Photo-Pictorialist Exhibition at the Albright Art Gallery set among some of the daguerreotypes in the collection of Robert McElroy, Buffalo, New York.

Collection of Robert McElroy

Photograph of Mrs. Wendell Endicott taken by Charlotte Spaulding.

Anthony Bannon, The Photo-Pictorialists of Buffalo. *Media Studies Buffalo, 1982*

Art School. Following what appears to have been a short visit to France at the turn of the century, she returned to Buffalo, where in 1904, the year before the gallery opened, she worked in the office of the Buffalo Fine Arts Academy. The following year she became the Assistant to the director of the new gallery. Her first initiative following Director Kurtz's sudden death was to resume the work that Kurtz had begun with Alfred Stieglitz.

Stieglitz, who had struggled to gain recognition for the work of the Photo-Pictorialists, was thrilled when Kurtz offered the Albright Gallery as the location for the first museum exhibition of what Stieglitz believed to be a new art form. The sudden death of Kurtz in March 1909 shattered his hopes. In a letter to Cornelia Sage written shortly after Kurtz's death, Stieglitz mentions the several visits that Kurtz had made to his gallery on Fifth Avenue: "Everything had been thoroughly discussed and virtually arranged to insure Buffalo of a really wonderfully fun and thoroughly representative exhibition." Now, following Kurtz's death, Stieglitz implored the acting director to continue the work of her predecessor: "With the hopes that the Albright Gallery will eventually find someone worthy to carry on Mr. Kurtz's work, I remain, Yours, Alfred Stieglitz."[14]

Stieglitz was not alone. Indeed, Kurtz's death, it seems, caused no small degree of concern in the world of photography. Writing a letter to the board of directors of the Albright shortly after Kurtz's death, the founder and editor of the *British Journal of Photography,* Henry Snowden Ward, urged them to continue Kurtz's efforts to mount, what he called,

Cornelia Bentley Sage's photograph was taken by Clara Siprell, one of the original members of the Photo-Pictorialists.
Archives of the Albright-Knox Art Gallery

a great international exhibition of pictorial photographers. No such exhibition has ever been attempted on such a line and if [it] could be carried out it would have an immense influence not only on photographers but also upon the great art world which has not yet realized the seriousness of purpose or the measure of achievement to be found in the work of the modern pictorial photographers.[15]

Stieglitz did not have to wait long. In a letter written shortly thereafter, Sage replied that as a result of "my personal idea" the Photo-Secession exhibit would open, as originally planned, in November 1910. But was her decision to mount the Stieglitz show really her "personal idea"? Could she by now have come under the influence of Susan Albright and Charlotte Spaulding? By this time both women had become increasingly accomplished photographers, friends not only with other members of Buffalo's growing female coterie of photographers—women like Rose Clark and Gertrude Kasebier—but also, it seems, with Edward Steichen.

There is something particularly intriguing about the relationship between Charlotte Spaulding and Edward Steichen. Both born in 1879, they met more likely than not at Alfred Stieglitz's studio and gallery on Fifth Avenue in the early years of the new century. Spaulding had begun taking pictures on her own, and as a member of the Buffalo Photo Pictorialists, she created several hazy and romantic images: *Sunset over Water; Branches over Stream;* and *Sweeper in Doorway*—each bearing the adolescent romanticism of the Pre-Raphaelite painters who were then so in vogue. Steichen, however, was well on his way to becoming one of America's

greatest photographers. Upon meeting him in 1907, Charlotte, although engaged to John Albright's son Langdon, undoubtedly fell under his spell. Steichen, equally stricken by the beauty of Charlotte Spaulding, demonstrated the power of his attraction by creating in one sitting two of the most stunning color portraits ever made. Soon after she returned to Buffalo, Charlotte Spaulding married Langdon Albright and never again took another photograph.[16]

Stieglitz, of course, was thrilled with Sage's commitment to the exhibition. In another letter he sent to her from his gallery, written in October 1910, one month before the opening of what was the first such exhibition in the nation, he said: "The show must be a real 'smasher' for your sake and mine if, for no other reason, photography is to gain a signal triumph. This show will be a revelation to everyone."[17]

Under the directorship of Kurtz, Sage, and then William Hekking, the Albright Art Gallery sponsored more than twenty photography exhibitions and became a major force in the recognition of photography as a major art form. The extent to which Charlotte Albright and Susan Fuller Albright influenced this is a fascinating and unanswerable question.

While neither Susan's nor Charlotte's work was on the walls, certainly John and Susan Albright and their daughter-in-law Charlotte were in attendance on that historic night in November 1910. Did Langdon attend? The Albrights were becoming increasingly close to Director Sage and undoubtedly supported her efforts. Mrs. Albright was chair of the Pageant Committee for the Golden Jubilee celebration that in 1912 commemorated fifty years of the Buffalo Fine

Taken circa 1907 by Edward Steichen, most likely in New York City, this gauzy and romantic portrait of Charlotte Spaulding, shot shortly before she married John J. Albright's son Langdon, suggests much while revealing little.

In the permanent collection of the George Eastman Museum and used with the permission of the Artists' Rights Society

The Golden Jubilee of the Buffalo Fine Arts Academy was held at the Albright Art Gallery in 1912. The photograph that appeared on the cover of *Academy Notes*, as well as those printed within reveal the lure of Neo-Classicism for the first generation of leadership at the Art Gallery. Taken in the style of the Photo-Pictorialist Exhibition held at the Gallery three years earlier, the photographs reflect the powerful influence of Stieglitz and his disciples in Buffalo. Charlotte Spaulding, now Albright, numbered among them. The photograph of what was then the front entrance to the Gallery is the most powerful and compelling. Taken by Oscar C. Anthony, a founding member of the Photo-Pictorialists of Buffalo, this image, with its hazy impressions, its suggestive and moody point of view, embodies the aesthetic ethos of Photo-Pictorialism. These photos, with their idealized, statuesque images of women, provoke other thoughts as well about art and life in early 20th century Buffalo.

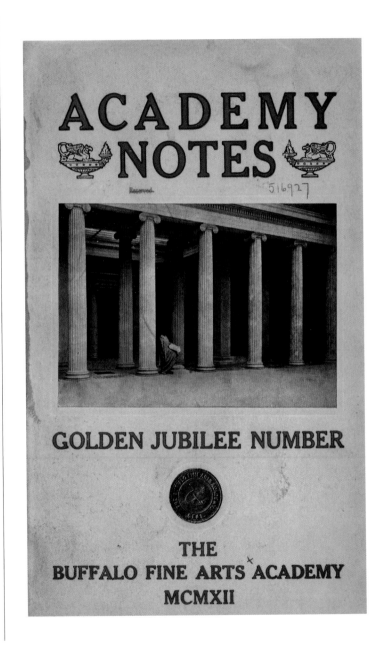

Arts Academy. Indeed, the program notes reveal that her seven-year-old daughter Betty danced the part of a "Flower Maiden" at what the accompanying photographs suggest was a fantastic event.[18] Certainly Susan, if not her husband, John, must also have been at the gallery on that night in January 1914 when Anna Pavlova, at the invitation of Sage, performed in the Sculpture Court celebrating the opening of a Leon Bakst exhibition that Miss Sage had curated. And were they not there as well when two years later Sarah Bernhardt, at the invitation of Director Sage, offered a series of dramatic readings at the Albright Art Gallery?[19]

By the middle of the second decade of the 1900s, John Albright was no longer playing a leadership role at the gallery. Although asked to once again serve as a member of the gallery board in 1918, he politely but firmly declined. In a letter written on December 21, 1918, to A. F. Laub, secretary of the Buffalo Fine Arts Academy, Albright said it "would be impossible for me to accept the nomination." He offered, not one reason but a mysterious-sounding many. "I regret to say that for many reasons it would be impossible for me to accept the nomination, and request that some other name is substituted for mine."[20]

Although no longer a board member himself, two of his sons, Raymond and Langdon, served— Raymond during the 1910s, Langdon throughout the 1920s. Albright senior must certainly have been privy to the issues and concerns of the gallery during this period. Of these, none was more significant or more controversial than the growing conflict among members of the academy's board of directors over modern art.

By the early 1920s, a new generation of leaders was emerging at the Buffalo Fine Arts Academy, men who shaped the future direction of the Albright Art Gallery. Particularly influential were A. Conger Goodyear and Seymour H. Knox II. Although younger than Albright by many years (Goodyear was born in 1877; Knox in 1898), the three men had deep connections that transcended their generational differences. Both Goodyear and Knox had come of age in a city in which the infrastructure of the modern industrial economy—the banks, the steel mills, and the power plants—had been created in large measure by the vision and the efforts of John J. Albright. Both attended Yale where, unlike Albright at RPI, they received a traditional liberal arts education. But both were also graduates of The Nichols School, which Albright had helped to found. While Goodyear's family was more closely intertwined financially with Albright's (recall their joint family "outing" to Chicago which led to formation of the Buffalo and Susquehanna Iron and Steel Company), Knox's family had been active in the Marine National Bank, cofounded by Albright in 1902, years before Seymour became a director following his graduation from Yale in 1920. The Goodyears knew the Albrights socially, as well, as members of both the First Presbyterian Church and the Jekyll Island Club.

Although linked through overlapping and interconnected business and social relationships (indeed, as a result of his sister Dorothy's marriage, Seymour Knox II was brother-in-law to Frank H. Goodyear Jr., A. Conger's first cousin), the Albrights, the Goodyears, and the Knoxes had starkly different views on contemporary art. That a significant rift in the board was emerging became fully apparent in the mid-1920s when, with Goodyear and Knox on one side and Langdon Albright and E. B. Green on the other, there erupted a battle royal—a full-blown *KulturKampf.*

As board members, Goodyear and Knox were pushing aggressively for a modernist agenda. Attempting to free his hands from a board still dominated by the Albrights, in 1926 Goodyear, anticipating a similar step that his protégé Seymour Knox would take in 1939, created the "Fellows for Life," an independent source of funds that would allow him to make independent and, therefore, bolder acquisitions. Goodyear, as chairman of the Art Acquisition Committee, added a considerable amount of his own money to the Fellows. He made a series of startling and increasingly controversial acquisitions, including works by Morisot, Gauguin, Epstein, Brancusi, and Matisse.

Prodded by Goodyear in 1927, William Hekking, the gallery's director since Cornelia Sage Quinton's departure in 1924 (Miss Sage had married in 1917), the gallery invited the annual show of the *Societé Anonyme* to Buffalo. It would be the only city outside of New York City to host the *Societé.* Founded by Katherine Dreier and Marcel Duchamp in 1920, the *Société* was one of the world's most persuasive advocates of modernism. Following this exhibition and using a combination of his own funds and those of the Fellows, Goodyear bought and donated to the gallery two daring purchases: Picasso's *La Toilette* and Matisse's *A Late Afternoon Glimpse of Notre Dame.*

Although neither correspondence nor meeting minutes exist as corroboration, this writer has surmised that the reaction among the Albright faction was more likely than not angry and swift. The stormy dissension forced Goodyear off the board in 1928. In a letter written eighteen years later, Goodyear recalled the turmoil that ensued following his purchase of *La Toilette.* Referring to it, Goodyear wrote:

> *The painting now in the collection of the Buffalo Fine Arts Academy (Albright Art Gallery) was acquired from the Quinn Collection, on the authority of the Acquisition Committee of which I was the chairman. It produced some very harsh criticism on the part of some members of the Board of Directors and others who did not like modern art in general, nor this picture in particular. As chairman of the Acquisition Committee, I was strongly in favor of building up a collection of modern art in the Albright Gallery.*

Goodyear suffered the consequences: "At the annual election of trustees following the acquisition of this picture, I was not reelected. A quiet campaign had been instituted by one or two of the trustees who were opposed to modern art to drop me from the board. This occurred in 1928."

While the Albright faction may have won that battle, it was Goodyear (and eventually Knox) who triumphed in the war over modern art. The following year, Goodyear, as he recounts in his letter, was asked by "three women" to "act as chairman of a committee to organize a Museum of Modern Art. I did not know any of the three women," Goodyear continued. But, he wrote, "The fact that I had been dropped from the Board of the Buffalo Fine Arts Academy for the reasons stated, I have been told, was my first recommendation to their notice."

By 1930, perhaps under the quiet but steady influence of Goodyear's protégé Seymour Knox on the board, feelings had changed, if not about modern art in general, at least about *La Toilette* in particular. When in that year Goodyear reported to the board of the Buffalo Society of Fine Arts that the newly formed Museum of Modern Art was prepared to pay $25,000 for the Picasso painting that the society had purchased for $5,000 just three years earlier, the board, with Langdon Albright and E. B. Green still members, rejected the offer.[21]

Through it all, John J. Albright remained an unreconstructed traditionalist. Alfred Noyes, the popular English poet and friend of the Albrights, described a visit with them in 1927 in the midst of the imbroglio over modernism. By then Noyes was living and lecturing in America. In *Two Worlds for Memory*, a memoir he wrote that year, he describes a visit "to see my old friends the Albrights." Albright took the Noyes on a visit to the Albright Gallery. "The splendid art gallery which [Albright] had given to the City of Buffalo" had, "passed out of his control." Albright, according to Noyes, was concerned—"humorously indignant" is how he described it—about some "modern acquisitions" made by the gallery.

The object of Albright's concern on that day, however, was not *La Toilette* but rather a sculpture that Albright told Noyes was called "a brass egg" (the artist of this work is unknown, and the Albright-Knox has no record of this piece). In an effort to "explain the work to us," Albright asked gallery director Hekking to

Picasso's *La Toilette*, the painting that triggered the "Kulturkampf" at the Albright Art Gallery in the mid-1920s.

In the permanent collection of the Albright-Knox Art Gallery and used with the permission of the Artists' Rights Society

join them. Noyes's narration of the visit offers a small, but nevertheless revealing, insight into the conflicts over modernism that were beginning to rattle, if not divide, the gallery. Noyes wrote:

> There it was, solemnly pedestalled in the center of much that was beautiful, a great brass egg slightly tilted to one side, and somewhere about the middle the faintest suggestion of an embryo human nose … The disconsolate founder of the gallery led us up to it … The director took Albright's request quite seriously and tilting his head to the exact angle of the egg, placed one finger on his forehead and in a deep earnest voice said: 'Well to begin with, it is an abstraction.'

Noyes could not help but notice his friend's reaction: he suddenly walked away, into another room. Noyes reports that when he returned, John Albright "was still wiping the tears from his eyes." Tears of rage? Tears of sadness? Neither, says Noyes. For now Albright, "able to see the fun of what the 'new age' would do to his art gallery, was laughing so hard that he cried." Noyes concluded his summary of his visit with a Sphinx-like statement about his friend: "I think he must have been the happiest millionaire…."[22]

While ambivalent about the direction that the eponymous Albright Art Gallery was taking, what is clear is that the "beneficent influence" that John J. Albright had hoped for was being realized. Albright's extraordinary gift cemented the gallery's place as the leading arts organization in the city and, in the process, laid the foundation that has enabled the gallery, first as the Albright, then as the Albright-Knox, and soon to be the Buffalo Albright-Knox-Gundlach Art Museum, to achieve its international reputation.

EIGHT

Family Memories

The photographs that Susan Fuller Albright took between 1900 and 1928 are extraordinary. They are beautiful and sensitive, intimate and revealing, detailed glimpses into the private life of a very private man: Albright lying stretched-out on a couch in front of a roaring fire in "The Chalet" at Wilmurt; Albright again, leaning casually against the railing of a trans-Atlantic liner; sitting, his right leg crossed over his left, on a wooden deck chair; playing cards with his friend Dr. Lyons on the terrace at Wilmurt; playing with this children, everywhere. At times Albright appears stoic, at other times, smiling broadly as he watches his favorite painter, George de Forest Brush, paint a portrait of his wife and children.

The photos that Susan Fuller Albright took of the family's safari-like journey to Europe, replete with their resplendent Locomobile, in 1912, are mesmerizing: Albright feeding the pigeons at St. Mark's Square in Venice; Albright and family parading proudly around the Tuileries Garden in Paris; Albright walking, his back to the camera, looking in casual wonder at the simple beauty of a Palladian courtyard. There are some group pictures, too. One appears to have been taken in southern Italy. In it there are five men, four of them looking directly into Susan's camera and one whose silent profile looks askance. In the center stands a scowling woman, her arms akimbo. And, standing in

John J. Albright bound for Europe, 1912.
Copyright Albright Family, 1912. All rights reserved

A few of Susan Fuller Albright's remarkable photographs taken during the family's European tour in 1912. CLOCKWISE FROM TOP LEFT: John and Susan Albright bound for Europe in 1912. The Albright's beloved Locomobile somewhere on the roads of Europe. Albright in St. Mark's Square.

CLOCKWISE FROM TOP LEFT: Villagers in Europe. The Locomobile has a flat tire somewhere in Europe, 1912, and Susan Albright takes an unforgettable photograph. The Albright family at the Tuileries Gardens, Paris, 1912.

Copyright Albright Family, 1912. All rights reserved

front of them all is a young, beatific mother, beaming joyfully at her sweet, slightly bemused daughter.

Even while travelling, Susan and John Albright were drawn to children. Look at the photo of the gaggle of children standing happily in front of Albright's mammoth Locomobile. There's Albright himself, barely visible in the background, standing with the family in front of the car. He and Susan were on the road and they obviously had gotten a flat tire. While they were at the side of the road, their driver working diligently to change the tire, a large number of children gathered around the automobile, perhaps at Albright's grandfatherly urging. Eager to capture this special moment, Susan, certainly with Albright's help, spontaneously grouped them in front of the automobile and, without missing a beat, took this extraordinary group portrait.

And then there are Albright's five youngest children, the primary focus of Susan's tender and embracing photographs, John J. Jr. (1898), Elizabeth (1899), Fuller (1900), Nancy (1905), and "Susie" (1907). The Albright children are everywhere and the Wilmurt albums are filled with them: three of them, two girls and a boy, posing happily on the steps of a rickety ladder in their Adirondack home; a shadowy portrait of a serious-looking boy sitting on a simple wooden chair in a simple wooden room in the summer house at Wilmurt, reading a book in the soft glow of the late afternoon light.

Birge was also right about the memoir *The Simple Life*, written by his Aunt Susie, the youngest child of John and Susan Albright. Susie was raised in the family's fabulous home at 730 W. Ferry. In the years

shortly before she died in 1995, she wrote a memoir of her childhood that was published in that year by the Albright-Knox. Describing the years 1915–1917, *The Simple Life* is an engaging and fascinating look at the dynamics of the Albright family, the perfect complement to her mother Susan's marvelous photographs. It is a memoir of growing up in the home her father built, a nostalgic and dreamy account filled with much joy and happiness but colored always with a sense of sadness and loss, particularly when describing the demolition of the deeply beloved Albright family home in 1934.

"C'mon," she says at the beginning of the essay, "I want to take you on a tour of the whole house and grounds from the top to the bottom. You need to know how I feel about it." She refers to her "dreams," which have, she says, "their own reality as I climb up the winding staircase and always stop on the narrow steps at the left while holding onto the iron railing with its delicate pattern and its shiny brass form at the bottom. Then looking up three stories at the skylight with the purple grapes and the green leaves that shine in the morning sun or shed a soft light on dark days or are almost invisible when covered with snow."

Her dreams are vivid and she wrote about them in the present tense: "When I reach the second floor, I never can decide whether to skip down the corridor to the right and dream about the blue-green wall painted in soft tones with Greek figures and temples or to gaze down into the two-story music room through the Gothic windows on the other side."

Susie was familiar with every part of her father's vast collection of art and she describes several works

CLOCKWISE FROM TOP LEFT: The "simple life" at Wilmurt (left and right photos). John J. Albright and Dr. Lyons on the porch at Arequipa, the Wilmurt lodge adjacent to "The Chalet," circa 1910.

Copyright Albright Family, 1910–1924. All rights reserved

Stevenson Memorial, painted by one of Albright's favorite painters, a New Englander named Abbot Handerson Thayer. The painting hung in the Albright's home at 730 W. Ferry from the time that Albright bought it in 1902 until it was sold at auction in 1926. Susie, Albright's youngest daughter, wrote lovingly about it in her memoir *The Simple Life*.

in her memoir. Her favorite was a painting by A. H. Thayer, a friend of her father and a member of the Dublin, New Hampshire, artist colony that Albright so admired. Commemorating the writer Robert Louis Stevenson, the *Stevenson Memorial* features an angelic woman sheathed in white. Albright's purchase of the painting in 1902 was newsworthy. An article in the *Buffalo Express* described it thusly: "Seated on the edge of a rocky mountain summit with the air of virginal dignity against a dark background of nocturnal sky, is the life size figure of an angel representing the spirit of poetry and romance, dwelling in the upper regions of rarified air."[1] The feature of the painting that so attracted Susie Albright was the woman's vast outstretched wings. Writing in 1995, fully aware that this painting, so beloved by her and her father, was sold at auction in 1926, she laments: "My angel with outstretched wings to whom I look with something akin to worship … My angel is beautiful and warm as she glides out of a black and mysterious background."[2]

Susie is a keen observer of the diurnal affairs of the Albright home, providing an around-the-clock account of the comings and goings of the household:

I am glad to note that the postman has walked to his wagon without a mishap this morning [he had apparently been nipped at by Sunshine, the family dog] and that his wagon has almost reached the gate to Ferry Street … I watch Tom, one of the gardeners, as he walks back and forth with the lawnmower. It takes him a whole week to cut the lawn … I also watch Bill—Billy the Lion Killer— whose job it is to pull out the dandelions by the root ... I watch Conrad placing the wood in the corner fireplace while Lena keeps close watch to be sure his boots don't soil the white rug ... I look out the side window and watch the elm trees blowing in the wind and I wonder how the orioles' nest can keep so safe when it rises and falls at such an alarming rate.

Still more intimacies are revealed: "I go back to the sewing room where the dressmaker, who comes often but is not one of the ten members of the household staff who live in the little rooms beyond the kitchen, is pedaling away on the sewing machine that makes a delicious, humming noise." She writes about the greenhouses:

We go to the orchid greenhouse which is in one of three long greenhouses ... I love the greenhouses ... We go out the far end of the greenhouses where we grow corn ... Just before meals it is rushed to the kitchen and eaten before the sugar turns into starch. Long rows of peas are ready for picking and I eat a handful ... We pick some currants and I plan to make jelly.

Susie loved the grounds of the family estate and knew, of course, that they had been designed by America's greatest landscape architect, Frederick Law Olmsted. In the spring of 1890, two years after Albright had acquired the more than nineteen acres of land that fronted on Ferry Street, he retained Olmsted to layout and design the vast space. Olmsted was familiar with Buffalo, having made regular visits since 1868, the year he was hired to design the city's park system

(the same year, incidentally, that Albright graduated from RPI). He eagerly accepted Albright's offer and, in an extraordinary letter to his client written in May 1890, Olmsted outlined his plans. In a sketch attached to his report, Olmsted called it a "preliminary skeleton plan embodying a general theory of design for your grounds." Seemingly responding to some of Albright's specific requests, Olmsted assured his client that he had "allowed a certain space for the new stable, a stable court, and a manure yard." In addition, he promised there would be ample room "for the gardener's house, propagating and grape houses, and a vegetable garden." Olmsted offered some ideas of his own as well, suggesting that Albright

... throw up in the north-west part of your grounds a ridge in the form of a horseshoe. Within this ridge there would be a depression of fine turf. The steeper part of the ridge would be planted with a continuous thicket of shrubbery, backed at some distance with trees, forming in this way a sheltered amphitheater [where Susie and her friends staged plays]. There would be bays of shrubbery and everywhere else would be flowering plants, mainly perennial, but with a good many spring bulbs. This would, we think, create an unusual and very agreeable form of garden.

With an eye to practicality, Olmsted wrote his client that his garden "would be easily taken care of and it would be more genial than most gardens in Buffalo." Most significantly, Olmsted concluded, the garden would offer a degree of seclusion that "would add a good deal to the pleasantness of the place." [3]

The recently completed Albright home at 730 W. Ferry Street
as it appeared in *The American Architect and Building News*
on December 15, 1906.

The American Architect, *Mark Goldman collection*

The Music Room in 730 W. Ferry Street, Christmas 1910.
Copyright Albright Family, 1910. All rights reserved

LEFT: Susie Albright with coachman Keyes, 730 W. Ferry Street.

RIGHT: A look inside the Albright home at 730 W. Ferry Street through the lens of Susan Fuller Albright.

Susan Albright Reed's memoir contains fascinating descriptions of Albright's oldest child, Raymond King Albright, born to him and Harriet Langdon in 1875. Raymond clearly was very close to his father. He spent most of his working life in companies that his father owned and/or controlled (at one point in the memoir Susan says, "Raymond is packing to leave for Bridgeport, Connecticut, where he is the president of the Locomobile Company.") He also lived most of his life under the same roof. At the time described in Susan's memoir, Raymond lived in his own "big apartment at the back end of the house. Albright, as we have seen, liked to keep his family close: Raymond in an apartment in the house; daughter Ruth and her husband, Evan Hollister, in the large and impressive home on W. Ferry that is today the Ronald McDonald House. Unlike her sunny recollections of the rest of the house, her recollections of Raymond's living quarters are dark:

[T]he apartment [is] of a rather gloomy man and everything in it looks gloomy to me, big dark furniture and big dark curtains that keep out the sunlight. The big, gloomy canopy bed is about three times the size of the canopy bed that Mother had given me for my birthday and is covered with some dark green material … a family picture sits on his big, dark desk with Mother (Susan Fuller) in the center.

Susie is at first struck by this. After all, she muses, Harriet Langdon was Raymond's mother, not Susan Fuller, the young Smith alumna whom his father had brought to Buffalo to help with the three Albright children. The photograph begins to make sense to her when she puts it in the perspective of family lore.

A family photo taken at 730 W. Ferry most likely by family friend Charlotte Spaulding in about 1906. Two years later Charlotte married Albright's son, Langdon. Pictured here from top left are Fuller, Jack, Susan Fuller Albright, Evan Hollister (Ruth's husband), Raymond, Ruth, John J. Albright and daughter Betty.

Susie Albright feeding the birds on the grounds of 730 W. Ferry Street.

Raymond, so the story goes, had fallen in love with his tutor, Susan Fuller, and in the years since had lived alone, sullen, and withdrawn, in the shadow of his unrequited love. Out of curiosity and concern she writes: "I look at Raymond and wonder if he feels as lonely as he seems to be."

While Susie was apparently unaware of the incredible photographs that Raymond had taken as a young man, she was very much aware of her mother's fascination with photography. She was, she says, "an excellent photographer," who "took pictures of every important family event in Buffalo, at Jekyll, at Wilmurt, and at the Farm." All of these, she said, "would go in the picture album at Wilmurt."

Susie reveals other interesting facets of her mother. She was, she tells us, from an old and very proud New England family descended, it is believed, from one of the original passengers on *The Mayflower*. She ran a strict and proper household and raised her children carefully and correctly. Susie recalls a time when she was sent to her room without supper because, she says, "I refused to go down in my new dress to curtsy to the dinner guests." Her mother is concerned about her children's elocution and is worried that Susie will try to copy the Irish accent of Mary, one of two upstairs maids, and urges her to do "anything to avoid the Buffalo twang." Susan Fuller was pleased with her daughter when in a school play: "[M]other said I sounded just like one of the New England Fullers and she urged me to stick with that." Her mother, Susie says, "keeps on hoping that her New England heritage will eventually make an impression on us." Despite her fondness for aristocratic New England ways, Susan Fuller Albright was not a snob. Indeed, she was admired among her friends for "her sincerity and friendliness and unaffected simplicity."

Susie loved what seemed to her to be the constant and energetic activity of the Albright household, particularly the many guests and visitors that the Albrights entertained in their Ferry Street home. "At dinner," she recounts, "it was not unusual for us to listen to Father's conversations with a variety of industrial developers who were in the process of making large fortunes or creating an art museum. They sought his advice, since the Albright Art Gallery had become a famous model."

Although only a child, Susie most certainly attended the "coming out party" that her parents held for her sister Betty in 1915. This occasion was apparently sufficiently unique and spectacular to still be remembered more than fifty years later when it was recalled in a 1972 article published in the *Niagara Frontier*, the same publication in which Birge Albright had published his essay ten years earlier:

The most beautiful entertainment ever was the coming out dinner dance of Elizabeth Albright. A preliminary supper was given at which Mrs. Albright presented her daughter to the older people. Then there was a party for the young. One of the terraces in the house was enclosed and tables and benches were especially built to fit in with the house. The tables filled several rooms and were lighted with only candles and centered with arrangements of fruit. The room to the right of the main entrance, known as the Flower Room with its marble floor and ceiling upheld by white marble columns was banked with masses of flowers behind the debutante and her mother. The great two-storied hall was hung with holly and pine and wreathes of laurel studded with fruit. A great fire blazed in the enormous fireplace. The dancers flickered in and out of the firelight and candlelight in the swing rhythms of the music."[4]

Overnight visitors seem to have been ever present in the Albright's W. Ferry Street home. Susie says at one point that she is reluctant to go to the west guest room where she might "run into a president of Harvard, a famous artist, or an archeologist and other visitors of renown who may be giving lectures at The Gallery." Edward B. Green visited often and was a regular at the Albright's on Sundays for dinner after church. Green seems to love the house that he designed for his friend and takes great pleasure in giving tours. Susie says, "If you ask him he'll bring the pictures and the architect's blueprints of St. Catherine's Court. He'll show us just where our house is almost the same as that wonderful mansion in Bath, England." Green, says Susie, "shares [my] father's delight in Tudor architecture, many details of which he has included in the design, most of them from St. Catherine's Court." Green particularly liked the main floor entry way, "the most majestic" room in the house. Susie describes it in shimmering terms:

From the high-ceilinged music room, through the flower room to the front hall and into the library, then into the dining room, comments of guests from all over the world have put it in a class by itself. Portraits and paintings by distinguished artists line the walls and the tapestries in the music room are forbidding with enormous knights in armor …

Albright and Green were great friends. Here they are sailing together at around the time Albright's home at 730 W. Ferry was being built, circa 1902.

The furniture is massive and elegant and the tap-estried chairs are for everything but sitting.

Green's favorite, Susie tells us, was the music room, "a place that provided the setting for large parties and, with its enormous fireplace, for Christmas Eve celebrations, or for a room filled with large audiences for concerts." It was a perfect room for weddings and it was here that three of Albright's daughters—Ruth, Elizabeth, and Nancy—were married.

In addition to businessmen and engineers, architects and archeologists, Albright enjoyed the company of writers, artists, and intellectuals. In May 1915 the Albrights hosted a lecture in their home by Professor Howard Crosby Butler on his Syrian archaeological expeditions. One of his favorites was an Englishman named Laurence Binyon who, by the time Susie wrote her memoir, was a director of the British Museum. Binyon was a poet and a scholar and, as "a frequent visitor," appealed greatly to his host. He was particularly well known as a poet and was the author of one of the most popular poems to come out of World War I, *For the Fallen*. Albright was drawn to that poem. He liked the romantic references:

With proud thanksgiving,
a mother for her children,
England mourns for her dead
across the sea.
Flesh of her flesh they were,
spirit of her spirit,
Fallen in the cause of the free.

On several occasions, Albright prevailed on Binyon to read it aloud.

Binyon was also an art historian who had worked as a curator of prints and drawings at the British Museum. What, specifically, brought him to Buffalo other than his friendship with the Albrights is unclear, but he seems to have blended easily into the daily life of the Albright family. Susie was particularly fond of him. She recalled happily that "he has visited us at Christmas and Easter. Once he took me on a 'tour' of our house. As we walked from the dining room through the library, then the front hall, the flower room and into the music room, he described everything as he would have conducted a tour of the British Museum."

Binyon also took the whole Albright family to "the Art Gallery," Susie recalled. "It's great fun when Mr. Binyon takes us to the Art Gallery; he has a way of making everything there come alive. He and Miss Sage are very close friends."

Another regular in the Albright household was an American painter and archeologist named Joseph Lindon Smith. Smith was from New Hampshire. At his home at Loon Point, he founded the Dublin Art Colony. Albright knew some of the regular members, including Abbott Thayer, George de Forest Brush, and extended family members like Mark Twain. Smith was noted in the community for his love of theatricals, and part of his Loon Point property was landscaped and decorated for these performances. It was this that both Susan and her father liked most about him. Indeed, so close was Albright to the Dublin Art Colony that, as a photo in Susan Fuller Albright's album attests, the Albright family once spent a whole summer there in a home they rented on the grounds.[5]

Portrait of Albright with daughters Nancy and Susie, painted by Edmund Tarbell in 1914 in the library of the Albright home at 730 W. Ferry Street.

Courtesy of the Westmoreland Museum of American Art

TOP: Susan Fuller Albright captures George de Forest Brush, paintbrush in hand, during the portrait process.

RIGHT: Albright is clearly enjoying watching George de Forest Brush paint a portrait of his wife and children in Brush's New Hampshire studio, circa 1902.

Copyright Albright Family, 1902. All rights reserved

BOTTOM: The finished portrait, much beloved by the Albrights, was donated to the Albright Art Gallery by the Matthews family in 1934.

George de Forest Brush (American, 1855-1941). Portrait of Mrs. John J. Albright and Children. 1902. Oil on canvas, 56 x 48 inches (142.24 x 121.92cm). Collection Albright-Knox Art Gallery, Buffalo, New York; Gift of George B. and Jenny R. Mathews, 1934 (1934:39).

Susan Fuller Albright, circa 1907. Could this have been the last photograph taken by Charlotte Spaulding before giving up her "hobby" following her marriage to Langdon Albright in 1908?

Smith was, Susie recalls,

one of my favorite men … [H]e writes and directs plays for us. He turns a lovely part of the grounds into an outdoor theater and the entrance in the back is between two large clumps of trees and bushes where changes of costume cannot be seen. The large white birdbath of Greek design is in center stage and the occasional appearance of pigeons adds a unique touch to the drama, which sometimes is an Egyptian scene … The audience sits on the wide steps that lead from the terrace outside the dining room and can seat over fifty people.

The attraction among Albright, Binyon, and Smith was mutual, each drawn to the other's dynamic, creative energy, and, at least it seems from the way Susie describes them, their sense of playfulness. Along with their host, they helped to create a remarkably creative and stimulating atmosphere in the Albright home at 730 W. Ferry Street.

Birge was not surprised by the mother-lode of material that I had found in his aunt's memoir. "She wrote another one," he told me. "It's about Jekyll Island. Go, read that. You won't be disappointed."

I found the memoir, also called *The Simple Life,* at the gift shop in the Jekyll Island Museum. Published in 1996, a year after Susie's death, the memoir contains recollections of her family's 1913–1918 winter vacations at Jekyll.

The mid-teens were heady years for Albright, the peak, it seems, of his prosperity. With a large and steady income generated by his family's ownership and control of two power companies—Ontario Power and the Niagara, Lockport, Ontario—there was little that Albright could not afford. And in 1913, three years after the infamous meeting at Jekyll that lay the foundation for the Federal Reserve Board, Albright bought the fabulous, 26-room "cottage" on the club's grounds that had for years belonged to Joseph Pulitzer.

"Jekyll," as insiders call it, is a small, uninhabited island a short boat ride off the coast of Georgia. With its miles of undeveloped beachfront, virgin forests, woodlands, and wetlands, Jekyll was the perfect place for an exclusive winter family resort. In 1886, a group of wealthy northern industrialists and financiers founded the Jekyll Island Club. Among the club's founding members were J. P. Morgan, William Rockefeller, and William K. Vanderbilt. Albright, along with his closest friend and colleague Edmund Hayes, joined shortly thereafter. Other club members from Buffalo included the Goodyear brothers.

While most of the members lived in apartments in the clubhouse, club rules permitted members to purchase individual lots and to build and/or own homes of their own. Albright was one of the fifteen members who did so. The Pulitzer-Albright home was one of the most magnificent on the island and it was there that the Albright family lived—they seemed to have stayed for months at a time—every winter from 1913 until the end of days. The Pulitzer-Albright home consisted of two separate homes connected by a gorgeous, sun-filled glass corridor, one of Albright's favorite sitting areas. Their home was a cherished place and Susan Fuller Albright took countless pictures of the family there: in and around their home, sitting in the glass-enclosed corridor, on the beach where, in

addition to swimming and sunbathing on the twelve-mile stretch of beach, they raced gasoline-powered small motorized vehicles, half-bicycle, half automobile.

Planning for the trip began right after Christmas and was supervised by "Soy," the Albright's major-domo. The German-born Soy was an invaluable member of the Albright household, responsible for many different tasks including serving as secretary to Mrs. Albright, governess and tutor to the children while on Jekyll (daily lessons were sent to her by Miss Keyes, the headmistress of the Franklin School in Buffalo), and German instructor for the entire family. Keyes, "the Irishman coachman," (was he related to the headmistress?) left Buffalo several days ahead of time taking with him the family's horses on a private horse car. The other servants, Soy and Dumbleton, the family chauffeur (the Albrights took their cherished Locomobile with them), traveled with the family.

As Susie recalls, travelling to Jekyll by train in private cars where "it was very luxurious to have our meals served in our own dining room," would take about four days. "The trip down," she wrote, "was a glorious change from the miserable storm and gray days that Father said would last until the ice melted in Lake Erie." Susie seems to have been a sensitive child, very concerned about the war in Europe and aware of the poor conditions of the people she saw as their train passed by. "The lonely little huts we passed at the edge of cotton plantations seemed to be surrounded by barefoot children. I wondered how people lived that way and why the children looked so happy as they waved at the train." When she asked her father about this, he offered an explanation that "did not satisfy me.

The "Pulitzer Home," the Albright's home at Jekyll Island,
shortly after Albright purchased it in 1913.

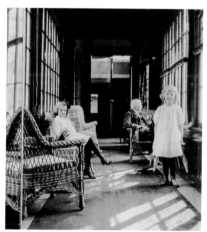

LEFT: Bike racing on the beach at Jekyll Island, circa 1920.

Copyright Albright Family, circa 1920. All rights reserved

RIGHT: Albright with daughters Nancy and Susie at Jekyll Island, circa 1915.

Copyright Albright Family, circa 1915. All rights reserved

Father said that they were happy because they didn't know anything else."[6]

The Jekyll Island Club was managed by one Ernest Gilbert Grob. While all of the service people—waiters, chamber-maids, and so on—were white, there were many African American employees who were hired for "labor-oriented tasks that did not require direct interaction with club members and their families." These jobs included road and forestry crews, construction of houses, livery men and gardeners. In an introduction to Susie Reed's memoir, the curator of the Jekyll Island Museum reports that in 1915, in order to accommodate the growing numbers of black workers, club members authorized the construction of ten cottages. Here,

> ... a community was formed that came to be known as 'Red Row' for the colors of the roofs. Each cottage measured 20'x 26', rested on brick piers and was equipped with a fireplace, stove flue, eight windows and an outside privy. With these houses, a gardening space was allotted and water was obtained from an outside pump. Other structures within this complex included a church, school and a grocery store.[7]

Life at Jekyll Island was lush, private, and, according to Susie's memoir, idyllic. But that all ended in 1928 with the death of Mrs. Albright. That, and Mr. Albright's increasingly failing health, brought to an end the family's annual visits. Following Albright's death in 1931, the family was forced to sell their fabulous Jekyll Island home for back taxes. When the State of Georgia acquired the entire island in 1947, the cottage was still standing. In 1951, a fire damaged the interior. Without funds to repair the damage, the cottage was demolished on June 23, 1951.

Alas, the good times and good cheer that Susan Albright Reed associated with her childhood in John J. Albright's spectacular homes were not to last. Outward appearances to the contrary, by the early 1920s the Albright family seems to have fallen on hard times, and in the years ahead, for reasons that are still not fully clear, all that they had began to unravel. Here too, as we shall see, it was Birge, ever vigilant and ever helpful, who would point me in the right direction.

NINE

Toward the End of Days

Although it is not clear what went wrong, there can be no question but that John J. Albright was struck by a major financial crisis in the early 1920s. Although his situation was made worse by the Stock Market Crash of 1929, a long and precipitous slide seems to have begun as early as 1921. If documents in Surrogate's Court are to be believed, at the time of his death in August 1931, John J. Albright, the towering giant of the industrial and financial revolution that transformed Buffalo, was penniless.

Like so much of the life of Albright, the reasons for his financial collapse are vague and unclear. There were very few public references to them. Even family members, grandchildren, and great-grandchildren, who grew up in the shadow of a larger-than-life figure that none of his living descendants ever knew, are mystified. Wasn't it Amzi Barber and the Locomobile? Or, what about those brothers from Cleveland, the Van Sweringens? Weren't they the forces that brought down this transcendent figure?

There was a short-lived recession during the early 1920s, but the decade in general was one of vigorous and vital economic growth. A rapidly growing middle class led to an incredible increase in the purchase of cars and trucks, homes and new products like radios and household appliances, all powered by the expanding use of electricity. Although the rise in the use of electricity led to a distinct decline in the use of coal, this should not have affected Albright; he had been out of that industry for many years. And although the 1920s were good years for the automobile industry in general, they were years of unprecedented competition, and many of the smaller, independent companies, like Packard and Studebaker, struggled to survive. While this might help explain some of the problems experienced by the Locomobile Company, it sheds little light on Albright's larger financial collapse. The sale in 1922 of Lackawanna Steel to Bethlehem Steel also fails to explain this collapse.

While we know that Albright played a critical role in bringing Lackawanna Steel to Buffalo at the turn of the twentieth century, I have been able to learn nothing about the nature and extent of his involvement in the company in subsequent years. Was he still involved when the merger was announced? How might he have felt when the company that he helped to birth was acquired by a steel giant like Bethlehem. While it is likely that he received little if anything from the acquisition (Bethlehem, it was said, purchased Lackawanna Steel for less than half the company's worth), at least he did not have to come up with cash as a result of it.

At the root of Albright's financial collapse in the early 1920s, his grandson Birge argues, is the deal that he made with his brother-in-law Amzi Barber twenty-odd years earlier. Albright's relationship with Barber began in Washington DC in the early 1870s. It was there that he joined him in the LeDroit Park real estate development and there, too, that they became partners in the Barber Asphalt Paving Company.

The brothers-in-law remained close even after the death of Albright's wife Harriet Langdon in 1895. In 1898, Albright was informed that Barber had bought the Locomobile Company, manufacturer of a steam-powered automobile of that name. While the roller coaster history of the Locomobile is of interest to students of automotive history, what concerns us here is how and why it was possible for Barber to lure the staid and steady Albright into what, to the contemporary observer at least, appears to have been such a preposterous business proposition.

Within just a few years Barber's Locomobile Company began to unravel. In 1903, with the company hemorrhaging cash and Barber in debt for as much as $400,000 (approximately $10 million today), he turned to his former brother-in-law for help. Barber's 1909 obituary in the *New York Times* explains the deal that Albright signed on to. The numbers are staggering. In exchange for titles to two "unnamed real estate deals," Albright assumed all of Barber's debts, $300,000 worth of Locomobile notes and $100,000 in cash. As if this were not enough, Albright agreed to even more: annual payments of $12,000 for the rest of Barber's life. The total settlement that Albright made on behalf of his brother-in-law exceeded $10 million in today's dollars.[1]

However, even this herculean rescue effort was not enough to save the company. Locomobile fell on increasingly difficult times after World War I. Albright, now in control of the company and desperately trying to save it, appointed his eldest son, Raymond, as CEO. At the same time he invested more than one million dollars in cash in the company, using proceeds from his 1915 sale of the Ontario Power Company. Neither this nor Raymond's leadership could save the company and in 1922 it was liquidated. This loss, Birge Albright argues, led to the disintegration of the Albright fortune that quickly followed.[2]

What was Barber's hold over Albright? Even in 1902, when he was so deeply committed to Lackawanna Steel, to building the Albright Gallery, to creating the enormous Ontario Power Plant, Albright was willing to come to the rescue of his former brother-in-law. This is particularly odd since it seems that Barber did not even need those funds. In 1906, he bought the "largest ocean-going turbine-propelled steam vessel afloat" and named it *The Lorena* in honor of his daughter. Later that year he acquired a mansion on Fifth Avenue in Manhattan for $500,000, the equivalent of $10,000,000 today.

The same question also applies to the gigantic loan that Albright made in 1923 to two other long-ago colleagues, the Van Sweringen brothers from Cleveland, Oris and Mantis. In addition to Albright's relationship with Barber, Birge Albright points to the relationship with the "Vans" in his efforts to understand his grandfather's decline.

It started with a real estate deal in the late 1880s when Albright and his long-standing partner, Buffalo lumber baron William Gratwick, bought a 1,400 acre tract of land just outside of Cleveland from the United

Society of Believers in Christ's Second Appearing, also known as "the Shakers." Hoping to create a luxurious residential community there, Albright's hopes were dashed by the deep recession of the early 1890s (yet another economic instability which Albright and his confreres had to navigate). Land sales and banking transactions ceased, and the land that Albright and Gratwick bought lay vacant and undeveloped. Into the picture came the Van Sweringen brothers, upstart railroad entrepreneurs eager to create business for their Cleveland-based rapid transit line. Around 1907, the brothers bought out Albright for less than a third of what he had originally invested.[3]

Although Albright undoubtedly followed the high-flying Vans as throughout the decade 1910–1920 the brothers assembled one of the largest railroad conglomerates in the nation, he had apparently no further business dealings with them. Then, in the early 1920s, the brothers, like Barber before them, called on Albright looking for money. The swashbuckling Vans were planning to build one of the largest and most ambitious downtown development projects in history. Their "terminal tower" in Cleveland would, in one enormous, interconnected structure, contain a massive railroad terminal, a hotel, and an office building. But they needed cash and they wanted it from Albright. Apparently still awash in money from his 1915 sale of Ontario Power, he agreed. In January 1923, he loaned the brothers $283,000 ($3.5 million in current dollars). It was this loan, in addition to his investment in Locomobile that, according to grandson Birge's biographical essay and some Albright family lore, brought down John J. Albright.

Other significant events were simultaneously occurring in the life of John J. Albright. John and Susan Albright had a long and close relationship with Cornelia Bentley Sage, the director of the Albright Art Gallery until she left in 1924. Both John Albright and his two sons, Raymond and Langdon, served on the board of the Buffalo Fine Arts Academy and were Miss Sage's friends and confidants, particularly Albright *père*. And, when times got tough for John Albright, it was to her, now Cornelia Sage Quinton, to whom he turned for support.

That 1921 was an especially difficult year for the Albrights becomes apparent in a letter written by Cornelia Bentley Sage Quinton in October 1921 to a gallery owner in New York City. "My dear friends Mr. and Mrs. Albright are well," she wrote, "but I must tell you that they have been having a great deal of trouble. They have lost all their money and have had to move into a smaller house: it doesn't seem possible but it is true. They are in a smaller house next door and it breaks my heart to see that this has happened." As a result, she says, "the entire collection of their paintings, etc., is in the Albright Art Gallery for sale." That this was a sudden, even precipitous, development is made clear by her concluding sentence: "This is not for publication and just for you."[4]

Eager to either prove or disprove Director Quinton's assertions, I moved my search from the Archives of the Albright to the bowels of the old Erie County Building where, in old and musty bound "libers," I was able to corroborate her claim. In a deed filed in May 1921, the Albrights indeed had transferred ownership of their massive estate located at 730 W. Ferry Street to Niagara

Finance Company, an entity about which I have been unable to learn anything.[5]

The deed is a very simple, straightforward legal document. No details of the transaction are mentioned: no price, no terms. It contains nothing about "the smaller house next door" and certainly contains nothing that might cast light on the feelings and emotions of the Albrights as the home and the way of life that they had created over so many years was no longer theirs.

According to another letter by Sage Quinton, written just one month later in November 1921, the Albrights had barely moved out when the new owners began to transform the vast estate that Frederick Law Olmsted and his son John had so carefully created years before. "Yes indeed," she wrote, "it is a terrible tragedy about the Albrights. The dear souls have not only moved out of their house but their creditors are now cutting a street through their beautiful, treasured property from Ferry Street to Cleveland Avenue."

Unfortunately, the creditors are unnamed, but the street mentioned by Sage Quinton is Tudor Place. In addition to St. Catherine's Court, another street that developers were carving out of the Albright estate, Tudor Place became the favored location in the early 1920s for some of Buffalo's newest, most lavish and most expensive private homes. The greatest intrusion right in the middle of Albright's once pristine property was the construction in 1927 of an enormous new home for John Oishei, founder and president of the Trico Company. What Albright's opinions were of Oishei, the windshield wiper manufacturing company that he founded, and the house that he was building

in the middle of the erstwhile Albright estate, however intriguing they may be, are unknown.

The sale of their estate was followed several months later by the sale of their art collection. During the summer of 1921, the Albright Art Gallery announced an "exhibition of paintings and tapestries collected by Mr. and Mrs. J. J. Albright." It was really a sale rather than an exhibition. More than sixty-five items from the Albrights' collected art were up for sale within the gallery. Prospective buyers were instructed to submit offers directly to Albright but "through the gallery."

Proceeds from that sale must have been disappointing. In 1926, they again put their collection up for sale and it, too, was displayed at the gallery. This time, however, sales were handled, not by Albright but by the Anderson Gallery in New York City. Sales were brisk. William Hekking, who had recently replaced Sage Quinton as director of the Albright, reported, "A very fine Hitchcock sold for $2,000, a Corot for $10,000, a Lhermitte went for $6,500, and a Jozef Israéls for six or seven thousand." Last, but certainly not least, a painting that had been treasured by the Albrights and loved particularly by Susan Albright Reed, Abbot Thayer's *Stevenson Memorial,* was also sold for the staggering sum of $25,000, $350,000 in today's dollars. The returns on the sale are impressive: about $50,000, in excess of $650,000 in today's dollars.

The timing of this sale could not have been better, because for reasons still not clearly known, Albright needed all the cash he could get his hands on. Indeed, it was then, in the mid-1920s, that he entered a cycle of borrowing that lasted until he died in 1931. Using the funds not for his own personal or business needs but rather to satisfy increasingly impatient creditors, in August 1925 Albright borrowed the staggering sum of $50,000 from a bank called the First Trust of Tonawanda.[6] While that loan appeared to keep him afloat for a while, in February 1927 he apparently needed additional funds and reached out to Fred D. Corey, a colleague from his Niagara power days to borrow an additional $10,000 (about $137,000 today). Then, in October 1927, at the same time that Hekking reported significant proceeds from the sale of his art collection, Albright borrowed $15,000 from a woman named Mary B. Barker, in Washington, DC, the widow of another former colleague.

Although apparently in the clear for a while, in January 1930 Albright was forced to borrow $31,254 from the Marine Trust Company, the equivalent of $440,000 today. While most of these loans were secured by pledges of stock in a variety of companies that Albright still owned, Marine Trust, the national bank that he had helped to found thirty years earlier, drove a harder bargain. Albright, they insisted, would need to seek and secure personal guarantees. However painful for him this must have been, he had to turn to some of his friends and colleagues, including Frank B. Baird, Jacob Schoellkopf, and Mrs. Seymour Knox.

Although this loan carried him through the year, it could not stop the bleeding. Beginning in May 1931, in what appears to be a desperate and devastating effort to satisfy his creditors, just three months before he died, Albright committed to a lengthy litany of loans: on May 15, 1931, he borrowed $10,000 from the Van Sweringen brothers, and on June 6 he borrowed another $30,000 from Marine Trust. That was not

Cornelia Bentley Sage Quinton at her desk at the Albright Art Gallery, circa 1920. Is she proofreading her letter about the Albrights?

Courtesy of the Albright-Knox Art Gallery Digital Assets Collection and Archives © Albright-Knox Art Gallery

TOP: Tudor Place: the subdivision of the Albright Estate, circa 1925.

BOTTOM: The 1920s saw the deconstruction of the Albright Estate on W. Ferry Street. Since the Albright home was part of the liquidation sale in 1934, it is not clear that Mr. Bell actually bought it.

Reproduction by permission of the Grosvenor Room, Buffalo & Erie County Public Library, Buffalo, NY

Albright Homestead in West Ferry Street Sold

Joseph L. C. Bell purchases beautiful residence which is one of city's landmarks

The former home of John J. Albright in West Ferry street, the history of which property dates back nearly a century, has been sold through the agency of Gurney, Overturf & Becker, Inc., to Joseph L. C. Bell, an attorney and son-in-law of the late Justice Herbert Bissell. The property has a frontage of 250 feet in Ferry street and a depth of 494 feet on Tudor place.

An ancestor of United States Senator James W. Wadsworth constructed a beautiful home of the Italian villa type on the West Ferry street site. With its rambling roofs, large tower and wonderful conservatory the house was recognized as one of the finest in the city. The late James Adam purchased the property from the Wadsworth family and lived in the house for a number of years before he sold it to John J. Albright. The house was destroyed by fire, but Mr. Albright constructed a replica of it on the site. It is the structure which was sold yesterday to Mr. Bell. The architectural beauty of the house and the spacious garden have long made it conspicuous as one of Buffalo's most attractive residential properties.

It is Mr. Bell's intention to remodel the house, making it considerably smaller, although preserving its principal features. The entire property will be offered for sale. Such portion not purchased with the homestead will be subdivided and sold as lots.

— Courier Exp. July 28 1926 —

enough, and on that same day in June, he borrowed yet another $20,000 from "the Vans." Two weeks later, on June 29, the Van Sweringens loaned him an additional $5,000, and on July 1, less than sixty days before he died, he went back to the brothers and borrowed $18,000 more—a total of $83,000 (more than $1.1 million today) over the course of just six weeks.

It was in the midst of a stage of baffled confusion over the mysterious collapse of the once mighty Albright fortune that Birge Albright once again reached out to me, offering yet another clue which, like the photos of Susan Albright, would help explain the inner workings of John Albright the man and his family. There were letters, Birge said, hundreds of them, housed in thirty-six boxes on sixty-six linear feet of shelf space at the Countway Library of Medicine at Harvard, letters that Susan Fuller Albright had written to her son, Birge's father, Fuller Albright. "Go there," he counseled, "ask for boxes 17 and 18. Let me know what you discover." I followed his advice and went to the Countway and there, in the wood and leather gentility that characterizes Harvard's libraries, I spent a full day poring over the hundreds of notes, card, and letters that Susan Fuller Albright wrote to her son Fuller.

Fuller Albright was an exceptional man. Born in 1900, he graduated from The Nichols School and entered Harvard College in 1917. Three years after graduating *cum laude*, he entered Harvard Medical School in the fall of 1920. While he initially took an interest in obstetrics and orthopedic surgery, the discovery of insulin drew him to internal medicine, specifically the study of metabolism. Following his graduation, Dr. Albright spent a year in Vienna studying with Professor Doctor Jakob Erdheim, one of the best-known pathologists in Europe. Upon his return in 1927, Fuller Albright began his residence at Johns Hopkins Hospital. And this is how he came to care for his mother during her final days.

Like his son thirty-five years later, Fuller was drawn back to Western New York during his last year at Harvard to write his thesis, "The Sanitary Conditions of Niagara Falls." It was an epidemiological study in which the young Dr. Albright detailed the working conditions and the quality of food production that occurred in the four Shredded Wheat factories located in Niagara Falls. Albright reported that "an unacceptably high incidence of typhoid fever and other infectious diseases" existed in the city, pointing at the "dumping of raw sewage directly into the Niagara River and Lake Ontario." How might his father have reacted to his son's report? Was he reminded of the hazardous conditions that had existed twenty years earlier at his steel mill in Lackawanna?[7]

But what drew me to the letters was not the extraordinary medical career of John J. Albright's son, but rather the hope that Susan's marvelous collection of letters might provide another lens into the Albright family like that offered by her photographs. By now, of course, I had become intimately familiar with Susan's remarkable collection of family photographs, taken as we have seen, in very rapid succession in many different locations over the course of many years. That discovery alone was enough for this intrepid biographer. But now, there were letters, too. Hundreds of them, written by the same hand that had taken those most extraordinary photographs. Would Susan's letters to her son help me to understand the mystery of Albright's dreadful financial collapse? Would they, like her sweet and intimate family photographs, pull back still further the seemingly impervious veil that shrouds the life and work of John J. Albright?

The first item in this perfectly preserved collection is a scribbled note from four-year old Fuller in which he simply writes "Dear Mama and Papa." The envelope, written it seems from the "RA" that is on the letterhead, by his older brother Raymond, is addressed to "Mrs. J. J. Albright, Waldorf-Astoria New York, NY" and is postmarked January 20, 1904. This is the only note from Fuller in the entire collection. Susan's last letter to her son, now Dr. Fuller Albright, was written on May 25, 1928, just three weeks before she died. Her doctor, she wrote her son, has recommended that she go "to Baltimore (to Johns Hopkins, where her son was in residence) and have my throat condition looked into … I certainly have felt pretty miserable."

In between there are thrilling discoveries, like the astounding postcards that Susan sent during a trip that she and her husband took in 1910, two years before their monumental world tour with the entire family. Illustrated postcards of the ocean liner, of small Italian towns, of a haunting "Arab street" in Algiers. Then there are the more mundane letters, written in 1916 and 1917 when Fuller was a student at The Nichols School. In one particularly interesting letter, written in the spring of 1917 from the Albright family home at Wilmurt in the Adirondack Mountains, she proudly recounts her son's excellent grades and in the process reveals a great deal about what young men at the school that his father had founded were studying:

Letter from four-year-old Fuller Albright to his parents, written on Raymond Albright's stationary in 1904, and a photograph of Fuller at about the age he wrote the letter, taken by Charlotte Spaulding.

TOP: *Copyright Albright Family, circa 1904. All rights reserved*
BOTTOM: *The Fuller Albright Papers at the Countway Library, Harvard University*

Postcards to Fuller Albright from his mother, Susan, while travelling in Europe with her husband in 1910. These postcards may be the only clues that remain from this trip.

The Fuller Albright Papers at the Countway Library. Harvard University

"Ancient history, Latin grammar, Cicero, Elementary composition, Greek Composition, Xenophone, and plane geometry." No matter where she wrote from—the Waldorf or the St. Regis in New York, Jekyll Island, Wilmurt, or her home at 730 W. Ferry, Susan Fuller Abright offered details about weather, travel conditions (on a trip home from Toronto in 1916 she complained that the roads were so bad—"Canada is spending no money on opening roads these days"—that they put their car on a boat to Rochester), and other activities and experiences along the way.

Then, from the time Fuller went to Harvard in 1917 and throughout the 1920s, are the steady, mostly unrequited, requests for him to come home and visit for the Christmas holidays. The first such letter was written in 1918, Fuller's second year at Harvard. In an endearing letter that Susan wrote to her son addressed to his room at Standish Hall at Harvard, she reminded him that when he did come home he should bring with him his "stiff collars as your Father and I wish you to have them for some occasion." He had obviously forgotten them on a prior trip, as she concluded her letter with the admonition: "Now mind!"

In 1924, Susan wrote: "In your letter you did not answer my question as to when you may get off, i.e., to come home." In January 1928, she wrote to Fuller imploring him to come home for his father's eightieth birthday party: "Wish you can come home for the birthday on the 18th. I wish you would telegraph me whether you are coming. I hope you can come."

John J. Albright's eightieth birthday celebration was understated and bittersweet. The Albrights moved back into their long-abandoned former home for the occasion and invited about a hundred friends and family members to a cocktail party late in the afternoon of January 21, 1928. "Lovely Albright Home Scene of Brilliant Reception," proclaimed an article in the *Courier*. The house, filled still with what art had not yet been sold, was "transformed into a veritable flower garden, with clusters of mixed garden blooms everywhere. Gift flowers were noticed everywhere and the guests were received in the music room with its two-story height and picturesque decorations." The Albrights were fully present, eager to greet their guests. "The host and hostess stood before the open fireplace, Mrs. Albright wearing a severely plain gown of black satin made on straight lines and carrying a corsage of mixed flowers of delicate coloring."[8] We can only wish that Mrs. Albright had brought her camera. That Fuller alone among the Albright children was not there is clear from a letter his mother wrote on January 23, 1928. "Your Father stood the party well and took a little walk with me about the place [their home on W. Ferry] today."

Surely, I thought, the trials and tribulations that the Albrights endured throughout the 1920s would be reflected in her letters to Fuller. Yet, a careful reading of her letters during what the record suggests was a terribly troubled decade for the family, reveals nothing. Indeed, life for the Albrights, these letters indicate, seemed not to have changed at all. In a letter written in August 1922, Susan writes, "Your Father and I went to the Gratwicks' for dinner and for the night. The weather was lovely and we had a delightful time." From there it was off to Wilmurt: "We took the train to Utica. Dumbleton (the family chauffeur) meets us there then in the car to Wilmurt." Later that month, Susan reported on a fishing expedition at Wilmurt: "Your Father caught 30 fish and is as delighted as he could be." In Boston, most likely to visit Fuller in November 1924, they stayed in "a suite of rooms at the Copley Plaza." Life, indeed, continued with no outward sign of change, let alone trauma. This from a letter written to Fuller in January 1925: "Virginia is sailing for Europe with her father. They are going to St. Moritz for the winter sports … Henry Erb called on Betty [Fuller's older sister] who went with him to the Country Club for a dance … Josh Dann's engagement to Emma Wykoff was announced today. Louise Urban is engaged to Charlie Crigni … I don't think there is any more news right now."

In October 1925, Susan sent Fuller a clipping from the *Buffalo Times* which reported that his 26-year-old sister Betty had opened a dance studio in Niagara Falls. It read:

> *Besides being one of the most popular girls at the college (she, like all the Fuller-Albright girls went to Smith) and a leader in all activities, she bore away the Phi Beta Kappa key. After leaving her alma mater Miss Albright was for a time interested in amateur theatricals. Her talent in this line was also marked. But it had been known for some time that her real interest is in dancing."* [9]

Eleven months later, in September 1926, Susan reported that she and Fuller's father had "motored" from Wilmurt to the Lake Placid Club for the Labor Day weekend. Despite the cold, she wrote Fuller, "Father seemed none the worse for it. He caught

"Beautiful Betty Albright" opens a dance studio in Niagara Falls, New York, circa 1925.

Reproduction by permission of the Grosvenor Room, Buffalo & Erie County Public Library, Buffalo, NY

Wedding of Nancy Albright and Lawrence Hurd, April 30, 1927.
A happy day in a difficult decade for the Albright family.

twenty fish and was much elated … He is now walking to the golf course with Mr. Foster of Buffalo." Writing in January 1927 on stationary that indicated that they were riding on a "Pullman Private Car" bound for Chandler, Arizona: "We are hopping off in a fine railroad car, each with a stateroom all in great form, with flowers, fruit, and books to make it all cheerful." The only apparent deprivation was that the Albrights, unlike their travelling companions, did not bring their own automobile with them. "The Pomeroys have their Rolls Royce here. The Bairds have a car here too, so we roll around the country with our friends." In April of that year, Fuller needed no urging from his mother to attend the wedding of his sister Nancy to Lawrence Hurd. Susan, writing several days later, thanked him for coming to "that happy and most festive celebration."

In 1928 Susan's letters to her son, although still laced with breezy commentary on the local social scene, are increasingly filled with her growing concern about the health of her husband. On February 18, 1928, she asked Fuller if he would meet them at their home on Jekyll Island. "I want Father to have a change of scene. He seems about the same but he has become quite dependent upon a nurse and could easily lapse into a bad, sudden situation. I think the best thing would be if you came down with us." When he did agree to visit, Susan wrote back, "Though your Father rather dreads the trip, he seems delighted over the thought of you getting there."

They returned to Buffalo in April 1928 and, for the first time, Susan suggests that perhaps she is not well either, writing simply, "I have been lying rather low since coming home." But still she has other things on her mind. "I suppose you know of Billy Gratwick's engagement to Harriet Saltonstall," she writes. And in this same letter is the more compelling revelation that, despite all that was going on in her life, Susan Fuller Albright was still taking photographs. In what is the only reference to her photography that she ever makes in this voluminous correspondence, she wrote: "Too bad they ruined my film in developing so I have nothing to show you."

At the end of April, she again returns to the subject of her husband's health. "Your Father seemed not to feel quite well. I discovered that he had a temperature of 101.5." Two days later he seems to have improved: "Father is feeling much better today and has been smoking in bed." A week later he "seems entirely well … He goes for long drives and walks every day."

It is not until the end of May 1928 that Susan makes reference to what must have been a rapidly worsening condition. She had apparently made a recent visit to a Dr. Burnham at Johns Hopkins where her son, Dr. Fuller Albright, was in residence. In a letter written on May 25, a mere three weeks before her death on June 18, she refers to "radium treatments for my throat and bronchial tubes." The results of that treatment were taking their toll on Susan and in this letter she asked Fuller if he would "please ask Dr. Burnham if he expected the result to be so painful and so lasting … I frequently can hardly speak."

And yet, despite the obvious seriousness of her illness and the great discomfort that it was causing her, life as she had come to know it continued for Susan Fuller Albright. On May 28, she wrote Fuller that she had just returned from the "last of the Junior League meetings with a large meeting at the Art Gallery. From there we went to a large luncheon at Mrs. Hoyt's."

But by June 1 Susan was in the hospital at Johns Hopkins "in the same building as her son and under his care." She died there, less than three weeks later, on June 19, 1928.

Susan revealed little of herself in her almost thirty year correspondence with her son. Given her reluctance to share even her medical condition with him, it is no wonder that she told him nothing about the increasingly precarious financial situation that plagued her and her husband during these final years of their lives. For she, like so many parents before her, was simply trying to protect her children.

It was more difficult to protect Dr. Fuller Albright from the details of the final illness which, in August 1931, led to the death of his father. John Albright had been suffering from an increasingly debilitating intestinal illness for years. While Susan did make a few casual references to his distress, it was his brother-in-law Leston Faneuf (married to his sister Betty), who provided Fuller with some of the end-of-life details.

Albright's condition worsened through the late spring and early summer of 1931. "Your Father has not been well for the last three days. He had scrambled eggs Friday at noon but couldn't keep them down," Faneuf wrote. In early July, in an apparent response to Fuller's offer to come home for a visit, his brother-in-law advised him not to. "He seems to be at a standstill, neither gaining or [sic] losing. Today he has called for you constantly and asked me to phone you. Frankly, I don't think much would be accomplished by your coming for he would confide in you about being

swindled, hold your hand while he goes to sleep and wake up not knowing you … As for family he has a dozen constantly on hand and by tomorrow he will have forgotten that he wanted you called."[10]

It is difficult to imagine Albright during these final, horrific weeks. His wife, Susan, had died suddenly and mysteriously while on a medical trip to Johns Hopkins in 1928. Although his children lived on or near Ferry Street, Albright himself apparently lived alone in what was described as a "small brick house" on the increasingly subdivided grounds of his once glorious estate. He was sick, having undergone surgery for unidentified intestinal problems during those frantic months of borrowing in the spring of 1931. How should we imagine those final weeks? Albright riddled with pain, paralyzed by shame and humiliation, making frantic phone calls, reaching out desperately to old friends and colleagues who might be willing to help? And why the need for such massive amounts of money? Who was calling him, pressuring him, during these final and clearly pathos-filled days of his life? What happened in those certainly darkened rooms where Albright spent the last days before his death on August 20 is unknowable. To imagine what they were like requires the skills, not of a mere biographer but of a supremely talented tragedian.

While we do not know if Fuller was at his father's deathbed on August 23, 1931, he most certainly returned to Buffalo for the funeral, the details of which, like so much of Albright's life, are unknown. Given what appears to be Fuller's relatively detached posture from the affairs of his family, it is not likely that he was intimately involved with the lengthy process that the settlement of the complex Albright estate required.

Shortly after Albright's death, it became clear that his children, faced with the crushing debts left by their father, had no choice but to dispose of everything that remained of their father's once seemingly inexhaustible estate. At an auction spread out over the course of three days in June 1934, the swift and strict hammer of the auctioneer, one Rundell O. Gilbert of New York City, just about everything that John J. Albright owned at the time of his death was brusquely disposed of.[11]

The low prices caught the eye of a man named Tony DeMarco who was in Buffalo visiting family when he heard about the auction at the Albright estate. The son of Sicilian immigrants, born and raised on Myrtle Street in the heart of Buffalo's east side Italian neighborhood. (Surely the DeMarco family attended programs at the neighborhood settlement house, Welcome House.) De Marco recalled hearing about John Albright as a child. He learned "to idealize the esteemed patron of the arts." He hoped that one day he, too, would have in his possession "such a beautiful and extraordinary collection of art."

DeMarco had left Buffalo in the early 1920s to pursue a career in show business. By the late 1920s and early '30s, Anthony, with each of his three successive wives as his partner, became "The Dancing DeMarcos," one of the most successful vaudeville and show business acts in the nation. Hearing about the auction, DeMarco hurried to the Albright home at 730 W. Ferry, where he bought "the lion's share of the art treasures" sold at the three-day auction.[12] He paid $95 for a carved walnut bedstead made in France; $60 for an antique marble bench from Pompeii; $75 for an original Hepplewhite card table; and $1 for a

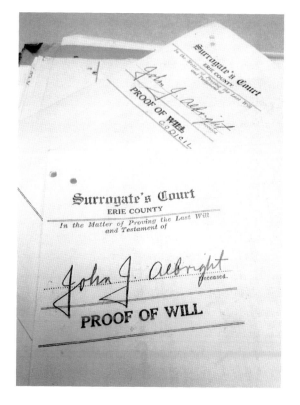

Will and codicil of John J. Albright
Erie County Surrogate's Court

Hogarth engraving. His bid of $610 for the gorgeous wooden panels that lined the walls of Albright's music room was the highest of the day. On the next day, he backed up three large rented vans to the front of the house, packed all that he had bought into them, and drove off, taking them, he said, to his "fourteen-room mansion" on Long Island.

Up for sale, too, was all that remained of Albright's art collection, including several striking Flemish tapestries, as well as portraits by the two great English masters, Joshua Reynolds and Thomas Lawrence. While Albright's children had no choice but to let these go, they desperately wanted to hold on, if at all possible, to two of their father's paintings that had deep emotional meaning for the family: George de Forest Brush's portrait of Susan Fuller Albright and three of her children, and Edmund Tarbell's portrait of John J. Albright with two of his daughters. The former resembles a rococo tondo, with Susan, posed Madonna-like sitting with her three cherubic children. The latter, painted in 1914, depicts a quiet, modest, affluent businessman, dignified and seemingly at peace with himself and the world.[13]

But there was nothing sentimental about this auction. The estate had debts to pay and complete liquidation of all of its assets had been ordered.

The Brush portrait went first. It had great significance for Albright. He'd watched it being painted, so lovingly captured in a photo by his wife, Susan. Indeed, to ensure that Brush had time enough to complete it, Albright had rented a house on the grounds of the Dublin Colony in New Hampshire during the summer of 1902. And now, like Tarbell's portrait of Albright and his daughters, it was being ignominiously sold to pay his debts. With no other bids offered for the Tarbell, Albright's son Raymond stepped up and bought it for $1,000. Moments later, an old family friend, architect George Cary, did the same and bought the Brush for $2,100.

On June 30, the auction moved to the exterior of the house and, in a tragic commentary that in many ways typified the personal tragedy that was the Great Depression, the *Buffalo Evening News* chronicled the proceedings:

> *First the shrubbery was put under the hammer. The entire shrubbery at the front of the house as well as that on the east side went to William R. Boocock for a total of $50. Then the seven skylights on the roof were sold for $15. The copper in the house, from roof to cellar, went for $20 to another bidder. The stone urns on either side of the entrance to the house brought $15 each. The flagstone around the mansion, 280 feet of stone balustrade, and the stone steps leading to the structure went to Edward B. Green, for $300.*[14]

But still, the article concludes, "Much of the exterior offered for sale went begging for bidders."

The Albright children managed to hold onto the house at 730 W. Ferry for several years after their father's death. In a letter to Fuller Albright, her brother-in-law, written in November 1931, three months after Albright's death, Charlotte Spaulding Albright reports that Albright's daughter Betty and her husband, Leston Faneuf, had moved into the family home. "The Faneufs have closed most of the downstairs using the upstairs sitting room entirely. Only the dining room and the library are still open on the main floor." In that same letter Charlotte, continuing the pattern started by his mother years before, did her best to convince Fuller to come home for the family's annual Christmas celebrations. "We are now planning to have a family gathering on Xmas Eve as usual in the big house. Though part of it is closed off as you know. Everyone seemed to want it there as it may be the last ever."[15]

Try as they might, the Albright children could not hold onto their palatial home. Too big to adapt, too expensive to own, too in debt to keep it up, and without a single potential buyer, the family finally and reluctantly had it demolished. On August 12, 1934, the *Courier Express* unceremoniously reported: "Tomorrow workers of the [ingloriously named] Buffalo Housewrecking and Salvage Company will begin demolishing the interior … Within five days all of the mansion is expected to be gone from the site. The cellar hole will be filled in and the ground leveled off."[16]

Christmas 1934, the first one after the demolition of their cherished homestead, found the Albrights at the home of Charlotte and Langdon on nearby Oakland Place. While the location may have changed, the spirits of the Albright family seem to have been hardly dampened by their experiences of the previous several years. In a letter to Fuller, who had missed yet another Albright family event, younger sister Susie, as breezy and casual as ever, wrote: "We had the Christmas party at Charlotte and Langdon's Tuesday night … Wats [Langdon and Charlotte's son] arrived in tails after strict "informal" instructions; Charlotte appeared in flame velvet and drank a full quota of champagne punch to live up to the stunning gown; Raymond [apparently still a photographer] showed delightful color movies of his trip to Alaska and then presented all females within sight with blue fox neckpieces for Christmas. All males received bottles of champagne which they did not empty into the punch bowl in spite of some persuasion. The party goes on."[17]

Epilogue

In February 1929, John Joseph Albright received the fourth Chancellor's Medal from the University of Buffalo. Created by University Chancellor Charles P. Norton in 1925, the award was given annually "to a citizen who has performed some great thing that is identified with Buffalo." The citation for 1929 reads as follows:

The name of the recipient is well known to every citizen of Buffalo. For more than forty years he has been a leader in unostentatious good works. The number and magnitude of these are unguessed even by his friends. Constantly in the measure of his capacity—and often that has been very large—he has contributed to fine causes here and in other communities. But especially he has fostered the instrumentalities of education, of social welfare, and of art. Two of Buffalo's distinguished schools owe to him their establishment. To this university he has made large gifts of money and of service. His contributions to charitable and religious agencies have been both magnificent and, true to the Scriptural injunction, for the most part unknown. But one of his great foundations could not fail to be conspicuous, and whether he would or not his name is associated with it and with this city for an indefinite future. Indeed, through its uniquely beautiful Museum of Fine Arts the prestige of Buffalo has been enhanced both at home and abroad.

But in making this award the Council of the University of Buffalo is not alone mindful of these large and numerous benefactions, it is mindful of a man whose personal quality is likewise one of the community's choice possessions. It recognizes not gifts alone, but a life.

The Council awards the Chancellor's Medal to John Joseph Albright, dauntless promoter of Buffalo's industrial development, generous contributor to institutions of welfare and learning, exemplar of Buffalo's highest standards of civic responsibility and of unpretentious social conduct, who has created for his city's fame more than one lasting monument and who not only through these foundations but also through a long life of simple greatness has "dignified Buffalo in the eyes of the world." [1]

How and what John Joseph Albright felt about this tribute is not known. He was not there.

All that remains ... the gates at 730 W. Ferry Street.

Photo by Mark Goldman

Notes

Introduction

1 Birge Albright, "John J. Albright," *Niagara Frontier*, 1961, vol.1, no. 4, 69.

ONE: Life before Buffalo

1 Burton Folsom Jr., *The Myth of the Robber Barons* (New York: Young American Foundation, 1967), 69.

2 Alan Teichman, *Leffert L. Buck Biography*, www.teichman-home.org.

3 http://pabppk2.libraries.psu.edu/palitmap/bios/roebling_washington.html.

4 Daniel F. Larkin, *John B. Jervis: An American Engineering Pioneer* (Iowa St. Univ., 1990), 27.

5 www.marktwainproject.org/biographices/bio_langdon_jervis.

6 Rayford Logan, *Howard University: The First One Hundred Years, 1867–l967* (Washington DC: Howard Univ., 1967), 47–48.

7 Beth Savage, *African American Historic Places* (Preservation Press, 1994), 141.

TWO: High Hopes in Buffalo

1 Buffalo City Directory, 1884.

2 Buffalo City Directory, 1890.

3 Josephus Nelson Larned, *A History of Buffalo, Vol. I* (New York, 1911), 238.

4 *Illustrated Book of Buffalo* (Buffalo, 1890), 102–3.

5 Liber 14261, April 12, 1887, 347, Office of the Erie County Clerk.

6 *Paul's Dictionary of Buffalo* (Buffalo, 1887), 19.

7 Ibid., 110.

8 Albright, *Niagara Frontier*, part I, 72.

THREE: Towards the New Century

1 *The Ontario Power Corporation of Niagara Falls, Ontario*, pamphlet (u.d.), Local History Department, Niagara Falls, Ontario Public Library.

2 Scrapbook Collection, "Charities in Buffalo," vol. 3, 275. Grosvenor Room, Buffalo and Erie County Public Library.

3 Catherine Faust, *Buffalo's Architect*, (Buffalo, NY: Buffalo State College Foundation, 1997), 16.

4 National Register of Historic Places, the Albright Historic District report, (n.d.) sec. 8, 7.

5 Ibid.

6 For changes in downtown Buffalo, see Mark Goldman, *High* Hopes: *The Rise and Decline of Buffalo* (Albany, NY: SUNY Press, 1983), 187.

For the Vitascope, see http://cinematreasures.org/theaters/20853.

7   John Sessions, *Nichols School: A century of tradition and change, 1892–1991* (Buffalo: The Nichols School, 1991), 26.

8   Ibid.

9   Ibid., 48.

10 Ibid., 49.

FOUR: Magical Kingdoms

1   For a general description of the luncheon and negotiations regarding Lackawanna Steel, see Mark Goldman, *City on the Edge: Buffalo, New York* (Buffalo: Prometheus Books, 2007), 16–17.

2   www.buffaloah.com/h/alb/steel.html.

3   Goldman, *City on the Edge*, 18.

4   Goldman, *High Hopes*, 7.

5   Goldman, *City on the Edge,* 29.

6   Ibid., 31.

7   Goldman, *High Hopes* , 32.

8   Ibid., 32.

9   Ibid., 141.

FIVE: Creating a Modern Banking System

1   *New York Times*, October 15, 1901, 23.

2   Ibid.

3   *Buffalo Evening News*, "A History of the City of Buffalo: Its Men and Institutions," 74.

4   Ibid., 85.

5   Ibid., 85.

6   Ibid., 88.

7   *Buffalo Commercial*, November 21, 1901. See Scrapbook Collection, "Banks and Savings Institutions," 73. Grosvenor Room, Buffalo and Erie County Public Library.

8   Ibid.

9   *Buffalo Express*, January 1, 1903. See Scrapbook Collection, "Banks and Savings Institutions," 224. Grosvenor Room, Buffalo and Erie County Public Library.

10 Ibid.

11 Larned, *History of Buffalo,* vol. I, 283.

12 Frank Severance, *The Picture Book of Early Buffalo* (Buffalo, 1912), 309–347.

13 *Buffalo Courier,* February 1901. See Scrapbook Collection, vol. I, 13, "Banks and Savings Institutions," 83. Grosvenor Room, Buffalo and Erie County Public Library.

14 *Buffalo Courier,* November 15, 1901. See Scrapbook Collection, vol. I, "Banks and Savings Institutions," 83. Grosvenor Room, Buffalo and Erie County Public Library.

15 en.wikipedia.org/wiki/Jekyll_island_Club.

SIX: Electrical Power

1   Larned, *History of Buffalo,* vol. 1, 152.

2 *Ontario Power Corporation*, pamphlet (n.d.), Niagara Falls, Ontario, Public Library.

3 Larned, *History*, 153.

4 http://vanishingpoint.ca/ontario-generating-station. For photographs of the OPC complex, see http://www.uh.edu/engines/epi2641.htm.

5 Larned, *History*, vol. I, 153.

6 Ibid., 154.

7 *Buffalo Express*, January 28, 1905, 11.

8 Larned, *History*, vol. I, 153.

9 *Buffalo Express*, January 28, 1905.

10 *Ontario Power Corporation*, see above.

11 Gale Evans, *Storm over Niagara: A catalyst in reshaping government in the US and Canada during the Progressive Era*, 2003, www.lawschool.umich.vol. 32.

12 *Preservation of Niagara Falls (H.R.18024)* Hearings before the Committee on Rivers and Harbors. Washington, DC, 1906 – (Hearings), 158.

13 Ibid., 106.

14 Larned, *History*, vol. I, 154.

15 Hearings, 161.

16 Ibid., 110–111.

17 *Popular Mechanics*, September 9, 1906, 933.

18 S. R. Fox, *The American Conservation Movement: John Muir and His Legacy* (Univ. of Wisconsin, 1981), 133.

SEVEN: The Albright Art Gallery

1 Birge Albright, "John J. Albright," *Niagara Frontier*, Winter 1962, vol. 8, no. 4, 98.

2 *Buffalo Express*, January 1, 1900, AKAG Archives.

3 Ibid., 11.

4 AKAG Archives (Series I).

5 Benjamin Townshend, *100 Years: The Buffalo Fine Arts Academy, 1862–1962*. (Buffalo: Albright-Knox Art Gallery, 1962), 13.

6 *Academy Notes*, Buffalo Fine Arts Academy, 1912, no page numbers.

7 *Buffalo Evening News*, June 1, 1905, 11.

8 *Buffalo Express*, June 6, 1905, Scrapbook Collection, "Buffalo Academy of Fine Arts," 45–46.

9 *Academy Notes*, Buffalo Fine Arts Academy, 1912, no page numbers.

10 Townshend, *100 Years*, 24.

11 Albright, *Niagara Frontier*, 99–101. Was John Albright involved as well in the management of the gallery's budget, which lists the following expenses during the first year: $1500, for coal; $500 for repairs; $100 for supplies; and $50 for the telephone? Under the "labor" line was the following: one "foreman" for $14 per week; "three men" for $12 per week; "two women" for $6 per week. Cornelia Bentley Sage received an annual salary of $1,040 (c. $25,000 in today's dollars). Director Kurtz earned an annual salary of $3,500

(c. $90,000 today). This information is contained in a memo at the AKAG Archives.

12 Anthony Bannon, *The Photo-Pictorialists of Buffalo* (Buffalo: Media Study, 1982), 11.

13 Ibid., 16.

14 AKAG Archives, Photo-Pictorialist folder.

15 Ibid.

16 Unfortunately, the Steichen estate has not given us permission to reproduce these fabulous autochomes. They can be viewed, however, in the Collections Department at the Eastman Museum in Rochester, New York.

17 Ibid., X.

18 *Academy Notes*, 1912, Buffalo Fine Arts Academy.

19 Thompson, *100 Years*, 26.

20 John J. Albright to A. F. Laub, December 21, 1918, AKAG Archives.

21 A. C. Goodyear letter, November 1946, AKAG Archives.

22 Albright, *Niagara Frontier,* Spring 1963, 102. The Noyes/Albright visit to the gallery was written about in the *Buffalo Evening News* on February 3, 1953, and was covered in Birge Albright's essay on his grandfather.

EIGHT: Family Memories

1 Scrapbook Collection, "Buffalo Fine Arts Academy," 42, Grosvenor Room, Buffalo and Erie County Public Library.

2 Susan Albright Reed, *A Simple Life* (Buffalo: Albright-Knox Art Gallery, 1996), 11.

3 The Albright Historic District Report.

4 Albright, *Niagara Frontier,* Autumn 1972, 72.

5 *Circle of Friends: Art Colonies of Cornish and Dublin*, exh. cat., Thorne-Sagendorph Art Gallery, Keene State College (Keene, NH, 1985).

6 Susan Albright Reed, *The Simple Life: The Memoirs of Susan Albright Reed at the Jekyll Island Club, 1913–1918* (Jekyll Island, Ga., 2010), 7.

7 Ibid., 7.

NINE: Toward the End of Days

1 *New York Times*, April 19, 1909, 29.

2 Albright, *Niagara Frontier*, Spring 1963, 95.

3 Herbert Harwood Jr., *Invisible Giants: The Empires of Cleveland's Van Sweringen Brothers* (Bloomington: Univ. of Indiana Press, 2003), 13.

4 Cornelia Bentley Sage Quinton to a New York City gallery owner, October 13, 1921, AKAG Archives.

5 Liber 1562I, March 31, 1921, Erie County Clerk's Office.

6 These transactions are listed in an inventory of the debts attached to the Albright file in Erie County Surrogate's Court.

7 John Naughton, "The Immigrant and Emigrant Albrights of Buffalo: Reflection on the life and

achievements of Fuller Albright, MD," private paper (AKAG Archives , 1992).

8   *Courier*, January 22, 1928, 11.

9   *Buffalo Times*, January 22, 1928, 13.

10 Leston Faneuf to Fuller Albright, July 7, 1931, Fuller Albright papers, box 18, Countway Library, Harvard University.

11 Courier Express, June 12, 1934, 11.

12 Undated, unidentified newspaper clipping, Albright File, The Buffalo History Museum.

13 Courier Express, June 14, 1934, 13.

14 Buffalo Evening News, July 1, 1934, 10.

15 Charlotte Albright to Fuller Albright, November 25, 1931. Fuller Albright papers, box 18, Countway Library, Harvard University.

16 Courier Express, August 12, 1934, 8.

17 Susie Albright to Fuller Albright, December 28, 1934. Fuller Albright papers, box 18, Countway Library, Harvard University.

Epilogue

1   *Courier Express*, February 22, 1929, 1.

Index

About the Author

The publication of *ALBRIGHT: The Life and Times of John J. Albright* celebrates Mark Goldman's 50th year as a citizen of Buffalo. A graduate of Brandeis University, Goldman earned his doctorate in history at the University of Buffalo. He is the author of *City on the Edge: Buffalo, New York, 1900-Present*; *City on the Lake: The Challenge of Change in Buffalo, New York*; and *High Hopes: The Rise and Decline of Buffalo, New York*, as well as *Max Meets the Mayor*, a Buffalo-centric children's book. To tell the compelling tale of John J. Albright, he embarked upon a long and circuitous journey, from small town archives to big city libraries, tracking down Albright descendents in New York, New Jersey and Massachusetts. He discovered hundreds of never-before-seen photographs and letters. For this illustrated biography, he employed a narrative framework rooted in inquiry to sift through the many layers of mystery which have for so long shrouded this enigmatic man. The result is a revealing story of one of Buffalo's most important and least known citizens, as well as of the turn-of-the-century city in which he lived.